Shakespeare Alive

William Shakespeare: A Man for All Times

Paul Shuter

Chicago, Illinois

To contact Capstone Global Library please phone
800-747-4992, or visit our website
www.capstonepub.com

Edited by Andrew Farrow and Abby Colich
Designed by Steve Mead
Original illustrations © Capstone Global
    Library Ltd 2014
Picture research by Elizabeth Alexander
Production by Victoria Fitzgerald
Originated by Capstone Global Library Ltd
Printed and bound in China by Leo
    Paper Products Ltd

17 16 15 14 13
10 9 8 7 6 5 4 3 2 1

**Library of Congress Cataloging-in-Publication
Data**
Shuter, Paul.
  William Shakespeare : a man for all times / Paul
Shuter.
      pages cm.—(Shakespeare Alive)
  Includes bibliographical references and index.
  ISBN 978-1-4329-9629-1 (hb)—ISBN 978-1-
4329-9633-8 (pb)
1. Shakespeare, William, 1564–1616—Juvenile
literature. 2. Dramatists, English—Early modern,
1500–1700—Biography—Juvenile literature. I.
Title.

  PR2895.S56 2014
  822.3'3—dc23   2013018038 [B]

Acknowledgments
We would like to thank the following for
permission to reproduce photographs: Alamy:
pp. 5 (© The Art Archive), 31 (© INTERFOTO),
69 (© The Art Archive); American Shakespeare
Center's production of Comedy of Errors
featuring Aiden O'Reilly, Luke Eddy, Johnathon
Reis, Ariel Jacobson: p. 57 (Photo by Tommy
Thompson, 2008); The Art Archive: p. 51 (DeA
Picture Library / G. Nimatallah); The Bridgeman
Art Library: pp. 22-23 (© Devonshire Collection,
Chatsworth Reproduced by permission of
Chatsworth Settlement Trustees), 37 (British
Library, London, UK / © British Library Board.
All Rights Reserved); © The British Library
Board: pp. 32 (C.21.c.45), 46 (Add.70438 f.18),
65 (Maps.M.T.61.(12)); Capstone Global Library:
pp. 6 (Trevor Clifford), 16 (Trevor Clifford),
17 (Trevor Clifford); Carlos Lemos@MOLA: p.
25; Corbis: pp. 29 (© Robbie Jack), 43 (© Jason
Hawkes); Getty Images: p. 19 (Archive Photos);
McCurdy & Co: p. 40; The National Archives,
ref AO3/908/13 (2v): p. 53; The National
Archives, ref PROB 1/4: pp. 66, 67; Paul & Jane
Shuter Ltd.: pp. 10, 27, 45, 68; By Permission
of the Shakespeare Birthplace Trust: p. 9;
Shakespeare's Globe: p. 35 (photograph by John
Tramper, 2012), 38 (photograph by John Haynes,
2010), 58 (photograph by John Haynes, 2008),
61 (photograph by Marc Brenner, 2013), 70
(photograph by Ellie Kurttz, 2012); Shutterstock:
p. 15 (© James Kingman); Superstock: p. 12
(Bridgeman Art Library, London); TopFoto.co.uk:
pp. 55 (City of London / HIP), 63 (The Granger
Collection); Utrecht, University Library, formerly
Ms. 1198 f. 83, now Gr. form. 12: p. 21.

Design features: Shutterstock (© R-studio), (©
David M. Schrader), (© Tribalium), (© tkada), (©
Valentin Agapov).

Cover photograph of the Droeshout frontpiece
to the first complete quarto edition of the works
of William Shakespeare,1623, reproduced with
permission from Getty Images (Rischgitz/Hulton
Archive).

We would like to thank Farah Karim-Cooper
for her invaluable help in the preparation of this
book.

The author would like to thank Patrick
Spotiswoode and Hilary Crain for their comments
on the first draft of this manuscript. Philip Hall,
agricultural valuer at Savills Banbury office,
helped me understand the value of the land
Shakespeare bought.

Contents

Some words are shown in bold, **like this**. You can find out what they mean by looking in the glossary.

Who Was Shakespeare?

In 1999, listeners to a British Broadcasting Corporation (BBC) radio news program voted William Shakespeare the "British Person of the Millennium." When the Chinese leader Wen Jiabao visited Britain in 2011, he said he had read Shakespeare's *King Lear*, and said Shakespeare was the greatest writer who ever lived.[1] People all over the modern world recognize the image of Shakespeare's face shown on page 5.

Many people who have studied Shakespeare's life insist that he did not write the plays that bear his name. Psychoanalyst Sigmund Freud believed the Earl of Oxford wrote them. Some great Shakespearean actors, like Mark Rylance and Derek Jacobi, insist there is "reasonable doubt" about the authorship of the plays. How can this be?

This book does not explore the theories of who wrote the plays. It is a biography—a form of explaining history. History is a subject that follows strict rules and acceptable evidence and how it can be used. In this book, we will follow these rules.

Myth   The Earl of Oxford Wrote Shakespeare's Plays

Some people say the facts of Shakespeare's life are not those expected for a great writer. The compassionate author of *The Merchant of Venice* would not sue people for small debts. Such a writer would not retire to Stratford, England, to "devote himself to houses, lands, orchards, money, and malt, leaving no traces of a single intellectual or literary interest." The Earl of Oxford, however, did go to college. He traveled in Europe and knew many of the places that appear in the plays. The events of his life fit with the stories and information in the plays. We'll revisit the question of who wrote the plays in the **epilogue** on pages 70 to 71.

The idea Shakespeare did not write the plays appears in films and novels as well. One interesting example is Elise Boach's novel for young adults, *Shakespeare's Secret*. In it, the heroine learns, "Shakespeare couldn't even spell his own name," so she decides, "Okay, so maybe he didn't write the plays."[2] This is fine in fiction, but it breaks the rules of history. In fact, six of Shakespeare's signatures survive, and he does spell his name in different ways. This doesn't mean Shakespeare was dyslexic or stupid. When he was alive, the idea of standard spelling didn't exist. He might spell his name in different ways in just the same way people might pronounce names with different stresses in different circumstances today. It is an example of an anachronism—using an idea from one period of time and applying it to another. This is always wrong in history.

This book will highlight myths, facts, and important points about the world in which Shakespeare lived. Reading the book will give you the evidence to come to your own conclusions about who wrote the plays.

SHAKESPEARE'S WORLD EXPLAINED

Money Then and Now

In Shakespeare's England, there were 12 pennies in a shilling, and 20 shillings in 1 pound. Pennies (called "pence") and pounds are still used today in Great Britain, but shillings are not. Instead, there are 100 pence to a pound. Today, £1.00 is equal to about $1.50 in U.S. currency.

Where Did Shakespeare Come From?

What sort of family did William Shakespeare grow up in? The first family member we know of is Richard Shakespeare, William's grandfather. By 1529, he lived in Snitterfield, England, a village outside Stratford-upon-Avon. Richard was a **tenant** farmer. He rented his land from Robert Arden, from the nearby village of Wilmcote. Richard was a step down the social scale from men who farmed their own land. He was successful and well thought of by his neighbous, often chosen to value a person's goods after they died. When Richard himself died in 1561, his goods were valued at £38 ($58). This was £5 ($8) more than the value of the goods of the vicar, one of the most important people in Snitterfield.

This is John Shakespeare's house in Henley Street today. The left half was the first part he owned. He bought the half on the right with two **gables** in 1556.

Richard had at least two sons, Henry and John. Henry became a farmer. John went to Stratford, as **apprentice** to a glover and **whittawer**. To learn a skilled trade, boys were contracted to a craftsman for seven years, living in the master's house or workshop, and receiving almost no pay.

By 1552, John was running his own business as a glover in Henley Street, Stratford. His house in Henley Street was half of the house now called Shakespeare's Birthplace.[1]

John was successful. In 1556, he bought the other half of the Henley Street house and another house in Stratford, which he rented out. As a successful man, owning houses and a business, John wanted a wife. Sometime between 1556 and 1558 he found one—Mary Arden.

The Arden Family

Mary was the daughter of Robert Arden, Richard Shakespeare's landlord. The Ardens were higher up the social scale than the Shakepeares. Robert owned a number of farms. He died in 1556 or early 1557. Mary was the youngest of eight daughters and wasn't married when Robert died. He trusted her despite her being a daughter and his youngest, and made her one of the two **executors** of his will. He left her his most valuable farm and money. Sometime after Robert's death, and before the birth of their first child in September 1558, Mary and the up-and-coming John Shakespeare were married.

Myth Mary Arden Lived at Mary Arden's Farm

The Shakespeare's Birthplace Trust owns a series of properties associated with Shakespeare and his family in and around Stratford. Mary Arden's Farm in Wilmcote is one of them. However, there is no proof this is where she grew up. A local historian, John Jordan, first claimed that this house was the Arden's home over 200 years later. He gave no evidence for his claim. Jordan made part of his living by guiding early tourists around the Shakespeare sites, and arranging for them to buy "authentic" souvenirs. It was in his interests to have another site to visit.[2]

Whether it is the actual house Mary grew up in or not doesn't matter very much. It was the house of a well-off family, and if the Ardens didn't live in this one, they probably lived in one like it. There is a video showing the Shakespeare properties on the Shakespeare Birthplace Trust web site (see page 78).

John Shakespeare's Success

John soon became an important man in Stratford. The town was run by a bailiff, or mayor, senior counselors called aldermen, and junior counselors called burgesses. From 1556, John had three junior jobs in the Stratford administration. In about 1560, he was elected as a burgess to the council. From 1561 to 1566, he was one of the two men responsible for the town's finances. In 1565, he became an alderman, and in 1568, he was elected bailiff, running the town. He was trusted and well respected. In 1572, John Shakespeare and a neighbor, Adrian Quiney, went to London on the town's business. They were given the power to make all the decisions that affected Stratford.

Historians often say John Shakespeare could not read or write. He used a mark rather than signing his name. However, Adrian Quiney usually made a mark, too, and we have letters Quiney wrote himself. So Quiney could read and write, but at the same time signed his name with a mark. John could have done the same, so the evidence is not conclusive.

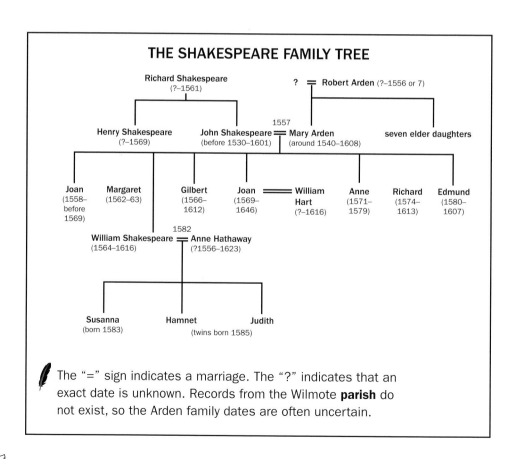

THE SHAKESPEARE FAMILY TREE

Richard Shakespeare (?–1561)

? = Robert Arden (?–1556 or 7)

Henry Shakespeare (?–1569)

John Shakespeare (before 1530–1601) = 1557 Mary Arden (around 1540–1608)

seven elder daughters

Joan (1558–before 1569)

Margaret (1562–63)

Gilbert (1566–1612)

Joan (1569–1646) = William Hart (?–1616)

Anne (1571–1579)

Richard (1574–1613)

Edmund (1580–1607)

William Shakespeare (1564–1616) = 1582 Anne Hathaway (?1556–1623)

Susanna (born 1583)

Hamnet

Judith

(twins born 1585)

The "=" sign indicates a marriage. The "?" indicates that an exact date is unknown. Records from the Wilmote **parish** do not exist, so the Arden family dates are often uncertain.

John and Mary's Children

The Shakespeares had eight children, of which William was the third. It is possible both his elder **siblings** were dead by 1564, when William was born. Joan, the eldest, died before 1569, when another daughter was given the same name. This was a common practice at the time.

William must have been a hardy child. When he was a boy, about 16 percent of children died in the first year of their lives. The first year of William's life was worse than most. Plague broke out in Stratford on July 11, 1564. Over 200 died in a town of about 1,000 people. One family who lived near the Shakespeares lost four children.[3]

William Shakespeare Was Born on 23 April 1564

Myth

April 23 is celebrated as William Shakespeare's birthday. People in England like the date because it means the country's national poet was born on St. George's Day, England's national day. Evidence of his birth date comes from the Stratford parish records, which show he was baptized on April 26. Churches believed in baptizing babies quickly, in case they died. Therefore, it is possible he was born on April 24 or 25.

WHAT'S THE EVIDENCE?

Baptism

A new law in 1538 meant each parish had to keep records, called registers, of all the local baptisms, marriages, and funerals. Some parishes, such as Stratford, kept quite good records, which have survived. The fourth line in the register under the year 1564 reads:

April 26 Gulielmus filius Johannes Shakespere

Years later, someone added the "XXX" to bring attention to Shakespeare's name.[4] The entry was written in Latin by a town clergyman. Translated, it reads:

William son of John Shakespere

In Shakespeare's time, people did not follow strict rules of spelling. His name is spelled in many different ways.

Elizabethan Grammar Schools

Queen Elizabeth I ruled England from 1558 to 1603. This period is called the Elizabethan era. Grammar schools in the Elizabethan era focused on teaching Latin grammar. Latin was the language of education, of learning, often of the law, and of international trade. It was everybody's second language throughout Europe. Men like John Shakespeare may or may not have been able to read and write, but they wanted education to give their sons a chance to rise in the world. That meant understanding Latin.

In Stratford, boys learned to read and write before they went to grammar school, at about the age of seven. School days were long: from 6:00 a.m. (7:00 a.m. in the winter) until 11:00 a.m., when they went home for lunch, and then from 1:00 p.m. to 5:00 p.m. Also, there were no terms. The year was broken up by holidays lasting one or two days, but school was twelve months a year.[5]

The school would usually be in one room, with the master teaching the older boys and an assistant teaching the younger ones. Discipline was harsh. Flogging with the **birch** was common.

Lessons

Rote learning, or learning by memorizing, was important. At the age of seven, boys had to learn three Latin words a day. By age ten, they would learn entire Latin books. Some of the things they learned was ideal training for a boy who would be a playwright:

- **Rhetoric** – speaking and writing effectively
- **Synonyms** – finding different ways of saying the same thing; for example, 150 ways to say "thank you for your letter" in Latin[6]
- Impersonations – writing in the character of another person; for example, writing as Queen Dido in the classical story where she falls in love with and then loses Aeneas, a hero from Troy
- Performance – in many schools, the boys did not only study Roman plays in Latin, but also acted them, which helped the students understand the plays

Shakespeare's education taught him a lot about writing, about the stories and myths of Rome, about **empathy**, and may even have started him acting.

FACT

April 26, 1564 William Shakespeare baptized. His father, John Shakespeare, was a successful local businessman.

After School...Marriage

We don't know when Shakespeare left school. The usual age to leave was about 15. We also don't know what he did next. We do know he didn't go on to higher education. It would be common for a youth from a family like the Shakespeare's to start working with his father, and that may be what he did.

His father probably needed the help. John was not only a glover, but also a wool **speculator** and a moneylender. In about 1576, when William was 12, signs of trouble arose. Having missed only one Council meeting in the previous 13 years, John stopped going. His colleagues on the Council remained patient about his absence, but they finally replaced him as an alderman in 1586. In 1592, John's name appeared on a list of people who did not go to church at least once a month. This could mean he was Roman Catholic, rather than Protestant, but the list itself said the reason was probably fear of being arrested for debt.[1]

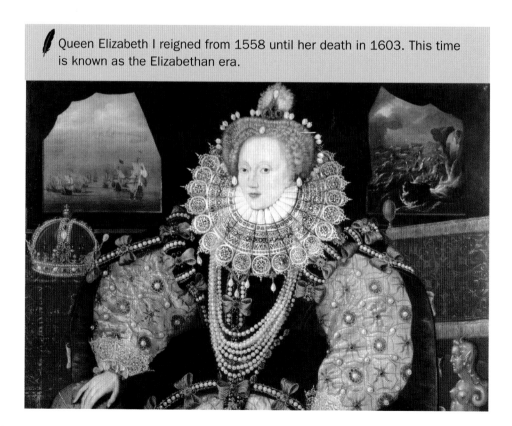

Queen Elizabeth I reigned from 1558 until her death in 1603. This time is known as the Elizabethan era.

A Catholic Family?

There is another reason for thinking John Shakespeare might have been a Roman Catholic. In 1757, when workers were repairing the roof of his house in Henley Street, they found a small booklet. This booklet is a Roman Catholic confession of faith, a list of 14 beliefs that Roman Catholics accepted, and Protestants didn't. For example: "Item, I John Shakspear doe protest that I will also passe out of this life, armed with the last sacrament of extreme unction."[2]

The booklet no longer survives. It may have been a forgery, but it could have been genuine. The text is very close to the *Testament of Faith* that secret Roman Catholic priests who visited England in the 1580s gave to their supporters. In 1581, one of them wrote to headquarters in Rome: "Father Robert wants three or four thousand or more of the Testaments, for many people desire to have them."[3] So a secret Roman Catholic might have a version of the Testament. Father Robert's would have been printed, not handwritten. If John Shakespeare could not read or write, then he couldn't have copied it. We can't be sure. And, of course, even if John Shakespeare was a secret Roman Catholic, it doesn't mean William was.

SHAKESPEARE'S WORLD EXPLAINED

Religion and Politics

Shakespeare's father, John, was born when the country was Roman Catholic. However, he lived through the **Reformation**.

- Henry VIII (1509–1547) broke with Rome and the Pope in 1533. England became Protestant, although a lot of old ideas were kept.
- Edward VI (ruled 1547–1553) made the country more strongly Protestant.
- Mary I (1553–1559) took the country back to Roman Catholicism. During her reign, Protestants were persecuted, and some were burned at the stake for **heresy**.
- Elizabeth I (1559–1603) took the country back to moderate Protestantism. Her government did not persecute Roman Catholics if they conformed. This meant going to Protestant church services at least once a month.

Politics were heavily involved in religion. Governments decided the people's religion, but many people's religious faith was more important than their loyalty to the monarch. Elizabeth avoided persecuting Catholics at first. After the Pope excommunicated her in 1570, telling English Catholics they should rebel against her, Catholic priests were tracked down and prosecuted for **treason**. In 1588, Spain unsuccessfully tried to invade England and make it Roman Catholic again.

Marriage

Men usually married when they were in their late twenties, and women were usually two or three years younger than their husbands. Arranged marriages were common among people like the Shakespeares. Parents, especially the woman's parents, often played an important part in setting them up. Once she was married, all that a woman owned became her husband's. Women usually brought a **dowry**, either money or property, to the marriage, and their father negotiated a marriage contract. This established what she would bring to the marriage, but also how she would be supported if her husband died first.

Before the couple could marry, they had to have the **banns** called. For three successive Sundays or **holy days**, during the service, the minister announced their plan to marry. This gave anyone who believed there was a reason the couple should not marry—such as one of them already being married—time to object. There were times during the year when banns could not be called. In 1582, this period ran from December 2 to January 13, 1583.[4] If people wanted to marry without normal banns, they needed a licence from the local bishop.

Shakespeare Gets Married

William Shakespeare wanted to get married in November 1582, but he waited too long to have the normal banns read. He was 18, very young for marriage at the time. To get a special licence, you needed a sworn document giving the names, addresses, and consent of all the relevant people. In William's case, this included his father because he was not yet 21, the age when he could decide for himself. You also needed another document declaring there was no reason why the couple should not marry and a **bond** promising to pay a fine if a problem was discovered later. If all the paperwork was correct, the bishop's court would issue a license allowing a minister to marry the couple and make a note in the register. This note appears in the Bishop of Worcester's register: "27 November 1582: [a marriage license] between William Shaxpere and Anne Whateley of Temple Grafton."[5] Temple Grafton is a village about 8 kilometres (5 miles) west of Stratford. None of the paperwork survives except bond: "28 November ... that William Shagspere on th one partie, and Anne Hathwey of Stratford in the diocese of Worcester, maiden, may lawfully solemnize matrimony together."[6]

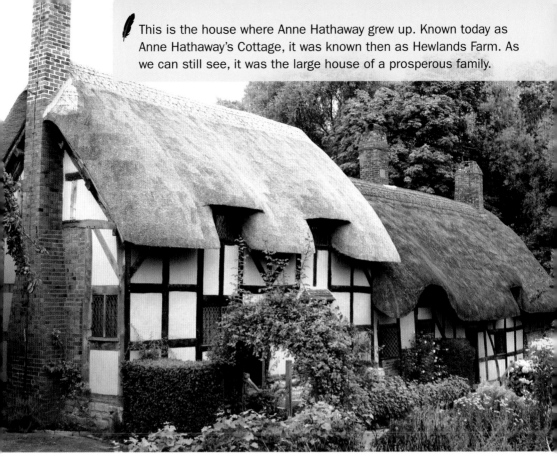

This is the house where Anne Hathaway grew up. Known today as Anne Hathaway's Cottage, it was known then as Hewlands Farm. As we can still see, it was the large house of a prosperous family.

Which Anne?

There is much evidence showing that Shakespeare married Anne Hathaway, and no evidence apart from the register entry that Anne Whatley even existed. William and Anne's fathers knew one another. Anne's father died in 1581. She would inherit money when she married. Her mother was already dead, so she was more independent than most women at the time. Her brother had taken over the family home, but Anne and her stepmother still lived there. She was older than William, probably 27, and she was three months pregnant.

The pregnancy explains the need to get married quickly, although it wasn't that unusual. Perhaps as many as one in three brides at the time were pregnant.[7] But how do we explain Anne Whatley? The most likely answer is that it was a mistake by the clerk who wrote up the register. He took notes during the session and wrote them up afterwards. Earlier the same day, there had been a case involving William Whatley before the court. Temple Grafton may have been the church where the couple were to marry.

Children

Soon, an entry in the Stratford parish registers noted: "[1583] May 26 Susanna daughter to William Shakspere." While Shakespeare's father may have had Roman Catholic beliefs, Anne Hathaway's family seem to have had **Puritan** ones. Susanna was a popular name among Puritan families, because of the story of Susanna in the Bible.[8]

Twenty months later, the parish registers have more news: "[1585] February 2 Hamnet and Judith sonne and daughter to William Shakspere". The twins were named after family friends, Hamnet and Judith Sadler, who were bakers in Stratford's High Street. Later, the Sadlers returned the compliment, naming their son William. As we have seen, Elizabethans didn't worry much about spelling, and "Hamnet "and "Hamlet" were two ways of writing the same name. Hamnet Sadler is also called "Hambnet" and "Hamlet" in the Stratford records.

Shakespeare's Birthplace is furnished with modern copies of old furniture and painted cloths. Here you can see the table, a bench, a stool, and a settle—a bench like a wooden sofa.

This jointed bed, with curtains for privacy, can also be seen at Shakespeare's Birthplace. Pulled out from underneath it is a trundle bed, for one or more of the children. The mattress rested on a network of ropes. When they started to sag, the bed was uncomfortable. The ropes could be tightened to correct this. The phrase "sleep tight" refers to this type of bed.

Home Life

Because William was so young, he and Anne probably lived with his parents at their house in Henley Street. This was John Shakespeare's workplace, as well as the family home. As a result, there was not much privacy for the newlyweds.

Today, an Elizabethan home would seem to have very little furniture. What there was would be handmade. It lasted a long time and was passed down through the generations. A family like the Shakespeares would have a table with enough benches, stools, and chairs for the family to sit around it. The seats were made of oak. People decorated the main rooms with hangings called painted cloths. These were made from linen painted with bright patterns.

FACTS

c. **November 29, 1582** William Shakespeare and Anne Hathaway get a licence to marry.
May 26, 1583 Susanna Shakespeare baptized.
February 2, 1585 Hamnet and Judith Shakespeare baptized.

What Happened Next?

We are now at what Shakespeare biographers call the lost years. In 1585, when Shakespeare was 21, the twins were baptized in Stratford. The next time we know anything about him, he was a playwright in London in 1592. Where was Shakespeare for the seven missing years? Unfortunately, there is no documented evidence to link Shakespeare with any specific job or trade during this time.

We do know he eventually became involved in the theater. Shakespeare was probably an actor before he became a playwright. Even his early plays show he had a great understanding of what worked on stage.

Myth
Shakespeare Left Stratford Because He Was Caught Poaching Sir Robert Lucy's Deer at Charlecote.

This story was being told in Stratford in the late-17th century—more than 70 years after Shakespeare died in 1616. Some people who knew Shakespeare might still have been alive late in the 17th century, but a 15-year-old in 1616 would be in his or her eighties or nineties by then. Because no one in the late-17th century was alive when Shakespeare left Stratford in the 1580s, there can't be a good source for the story. Additionally, Sir Robert Lucy did not have a deer park in Charlecote in the 1580s. There was one, however, in the 1680s when the story was first recorded.

Later, visitors to Stratford were often told Shakespeare drank a lot. One story tells that he got so drunk in a village outside Stratford, that he was unable to walk home and had to sleep under a tree. For a fee, a guide would show them the tree or sell them a souvenir cut from it. Such legends suggest that local people know the "real" person. People may have come from London wanting to know about Shakespeare the great writer, but people in Stratford said they knew the real Shakespeare. The one they know was a "good lad"—drinking, poaching, and getting into trouble like some other young men.

Myths about Shakespeare, like the poaching story, are often believed. Some Shakespeare biographers make the stories part of his life. This illustration shows Shakespeare (second from left, standing) caught with the deer. Strangely, Shakespeare seems to be wearing his best clothes.

When Did Shakespeare First See Professional Plays?

In the 1560s, there were no permanent theaters. Professional actors belonged to companies funded by noble **patrons**. They performed at their patrons' homes. The best actors performed at the queen's **court**. They also toured around the country. These traveling players often visited Stratford. We know this because the town's records show that money was paid to them. Traveling players made a grand entrance when they arrived in a town, then marched to the mayor's house. They showed the mayor their license from their patron, and asked permission to perform in the town. In 1569, when Shakespeare was five, his father was the bailiff, so the procession would have come to his home. A boy also born in 1564 described an event like this in nearby Gloucester:

> *My father took me with him, and made me stand between his legs, as he sat on one of the benches, where we saw and heard very well. This sight took such an impression on me that [years later] it was as fresh in my memory as if I had seen it newly acted.*[2]

Filling the Lost Years

In 1592, Shakespeare was a man of the theater in London. In 1583 and 1585, he was a young husband and father in Stratford. Biographers have a problem. They look for explanations of how this change happened. Those who believe the poaching myth often believe another myth—that Shakespeare's first job in the theater was as a horse-holder. This was the equivalent of a modern valet-parking attendant. Some people believe Shakespeare was a lawyer's clerk or a soldier because his plays reflect a knowledge of law and warfare. Let's take a look at the two most popular theories that might explain Shakespeare's success in the theater.

WHAT'S THE EVIDENCE?

Was Shakespeare in Lancashire?

Shakespeare's last master at Stratford school was a Lancashire man with Catholic connections. Perhaps he knew Shakespeare's father was a secret Catholic, and he got Shakespeare a job as a private tutor or even an actor with a Lancashire Catholic family.

- In 1581, Alexander Hoghton, a Lancashire Catholic gentleman, made a will which mentioned two actors and musicians in his service: one was "William Shakeshafte."
- Hoghton had connections with Lord Strange, whose estates were in Lancashire, and who had a company of players called Strange's Men that were one of the main companies in London.
- Strange's Men may have played some of Shakespeare's early plays.

This theory might be possible. However, the only real evidence, the mention of Shakeshafte, is weak.

- William Shakespeare's name is spelled in many different ways, but this would be the only time it was spelled as "Shakeshafte."
- Shakeshafte was a common Lancashire surname, and there were several families with that name in Preston, the nearest town to Hoghton's estate.
- Shakespeare was only 17 in 1581, which makes him very young to be an important actor mentioned in Hoghton's will. We also know he was back in Stratford in 1582, marrying Anne Hathaway.

Did He Join a Group of Traveling Players?

We know traveling players visited Stratford. At some point, Shakespeare got to know some of them. He joined a company, probably as an actor, and, when the company went to London, so did Shakespeare. There is no hard evidence to prove this theory, but there is evidence that may support, rather than prove, it.

◆ In 1587, the most famous company, the Queen's Men, toured Oxfordshire and Warwickshire. On June 13, one of its main actors was killed in a fight with another member of the company in Thame, Oxfordshire. They needed a new actor.

◆ Shakespeare was connected with members of the Queen's Men later in his career, including John Heminges, who was close to Shakespeare for the rest of his working life and is one of the two men responsible for publishing Shakespeare's plays after his death.

◆ Some of Shakespeare's plays, including *King Lear, Richard III,* and *Henry V,* are rewrites of plays the Queen's Men performed in the 1580s.

London

However he got there, by 1592 Shakespeare was a successful playwright in London. Scholars still hope to find the evidence that solves the puzzle of the lost years. They may never succeed. Shakespeare certainly understood what worked on the stage. Actors and directors today say even his early plays show this. This means it is likely that he was an actor first, and then a playwright.

London's first playhouses, the Theatre (built by James Burbage, 1576) and the Curtain (the tall building at center-left, built nearby, c. 1577), were built just outside the city because London's mayor and Council disapproved.

Moving to London

Shakespeare came to London in his early 20s, during the second half of the 1580s. What was the city like?

London

Around 1600, London was by far the largest city in England. About 200,000 people lived there, which made it more than 10 times larger than the next biggest cities. It was the center of the nation's government and the heart of its economy. Westminster, where laws were made and home of the royal court, was only a couple of miles down the Thames River from London (left, in the picture below). London was England's biggest and busiest port, with the largest ships able to dock anywhere east of the bridge (right, below). It was also the most important manufacturing city in the country.

London grew, both in population and in area, throughout Shakespeare's lifetime. Before the Reformation, there were many monasteries and other religious buildings inside the city, as well as St. Paul's Cathedral, and over 100 parish churches. After the Reformation, the new Church of England only used the churches and the Cathedral. King Henry VIII took the monasteries and other church lands and sold or gave them away. At this time, London had property developers just like modern London, and they flourished in the old church lands. Much of this land was just outside the old city walls, in the areas called the suburbs, so most of it was outside the control of the mayor and Council. Called "liberties," they are where the first theaters were built.

What Did London Look Like?

A Dutch artist painted the picture below, probably in the 1620s, although he may never have personally seen London. He was copying an engraving published in 1616 by another Dutchman, Claes Visscher. Visscher probably never saw London either. He based his engraving on one by John Norden, drawn around 1600. So this painting is a copy of a copy. It has mistakes, but it gives us a good idea of the city about 10 years after Shakespeare arrived.

This painting shows London from the south, and it illustrates how important the river was to the city. The Tower of London, with its four domed towers, stands to the right. It was a multi-purpose royal site—fortress, prison, royal palace, mint, **armory**, jewel house, and record storage facility. Ordinary citizens could get married there and visit the Tower's zoo.

The bridge was about 800 feet (244 meters) long, with houses built on arches above the roadway. The lower floors of these houses were shops that opened onto the road. There were only three gaps between the shops where you could see the river at all.

St. Paul's Cathedral dominates the center of the painting. It was a great gothic structure later destroyed in the Great Fire of London in 1666. It was more than just a church. In the nave, lawyers met their clients, servants looked for employers, fashionable young men walked about to show off their latest clothes, and tailors displayed their cloth and lace. Delivery men even used it as a shortcut. Outside, the churchyard was the center of the book industry.

The London Theaters

When Shakespeare joined the industry, acting companies toured the country, playing in the bigger towns, and in London, usually in inns. The best acting companies also performed for the queen. London, with its large population, was the best place for them, but the mayor and Council tried to keep them out.

To get round the city's opposition, and to avoid splitting the profits with the innkeepers, businessmen built special playhouses, in liberties and suburbs. The most important early ones were the Theatre (1576) and the Curtain (1577), both north of the city. Later, the Rose (1587), the Swan (1595), and the Globe (1599) were built south of the river in an area called Bankside. Theaters were normally built by businessmen, because they needed **capital** to pay the costs of renting or buying the land and paying for the building. The businessman then needed a deal with a playing company to perform in his theater. The money from ticket sales was shared between the businessman and the company.

What were these buildings like? Each one was slightly different, but they had common features. They were **polygonal**. In the center was an open-air yard, where some of the audience stood to watch the play. Jutting into the yard was the stage, perhaps 5 feet (1.5 m) high. Around the yard were roofed **galleries**, usually three stories, providing seats, and open on the yard side. Behind the stage was the **tiring house**, where the actors changed and stored their costumes and props. The front of the tiring house was the back wall of the stage. There were usually three doors, one on each side, and a larger one in the middle. They were made from a timber frame, with the outside walls filled in with **lath and plaster**. Thomas Platter, a Swiss tourist, described them in his journal:

They play on a raised stage, so that everyone has a good view. There are different galleries where the seating is better and more comfortable and therefore more expensive. Those who stand below only pay one English penny, but if you wish to sit, you enter by another door, and pay another penny. If you want to sit in the most comfortable (cushioned) seats, where you not only see everything well, but also can be seen, then you pay yet another penny, at another door. During the performance, food and drink are carried round the audience, so that, for what one cares to pay, one may have refreshment.[1]

The Archaeology of the Rose Theater

In 1888–1889, archaeologists found the remains of the Rose theater. In the plan below, those things marked in black were found, and the lighter lines are what archaeologists infer were there. The entire right-hand side of the Rose is unexcavated. You can see the Rose was a 14-sided polygon (it was not possible to make a circular timber-framed building). The yard sloped towards the stage, both for drainage and to help the people at the back get a better view. The remains can't tell us about the back wall of the stage. In the drawing, it has been left as a timber framework, but it would certainly have been a solid wall with doors. The owners sold food and drink to the playgoers from the building called Cholmley's house.[2]

How Do We Know Shakespeare Was an Actor and Playwright?

The "lost years" end in 1592, when Shakespeare is mentioned in a pamphlet called *Greene's Groats-worth of Witte, bought with a million of repentance. Describing the folly of youth, the falsehood of makeshift flatterers, the misery of the negligent, and mischiefs of deceiving courtesans. Written before his death and published at his dying request.* The book attacked many people, including both Christopher Marlowe and Shakespeare. This is what it says about Shakespeare:

> *there is an upstart Crow, beautified with our feathers, that with his* Tygers hart wrapt in a Players hide, *supposes he is as well able to bombast out a blanke verse as the best of you: and being an absolute* Johannes fac totum, *is in his owne conceit the onely Shake-scene in a countrie.*[3]

This description of Shakespeare was very unkind.

- "Upstart" suggests both a very recent success, and that Shakespeare was from a lower social class, or not well educated, unlike Greene and his university-educated friends.
- The crow was thought to only be able to imitate other birds, not make up its own song. Here it means actor, because actors say other people's words ("our feathers").

SHAKESPEARE'S WORLD EXPLAINED

Marlowe's Mighty Line

The star company of actors in the 1580s were the Queen's Men. Their plays were in verse, which often rhymed. In the late 1580s, new playwrights burst onto the scene, writing a new kind of verse. The most successful was Christopher Marlowe. His new verse, called blank verse, didn't rhyme. The lines were shorter, too. The older plays often used a 14-syllable line, but Marlowe used ten. This is called an iambic pentameter—a line of five pairs of syllables, with the second syllable subtly stressed. The first three lines from Marlowe's first great hit, *Tamburlaine*, show how it worked. Stress the bold parts as you read:

From **jigg**ing **veins** of **rhy**ming **mo**ther-**wits**,
And **such** con**ceits** as **clow**nage **keeps** in **pay**,
We'll **lead** you **to** the **state**ly **tent** of **war**.

The words mean no more rhymes and no more clowns, but instead a thrilling story of war and conquest. Shakespeare, who wrote his first plays around the same time, was one of the men writing the new blank verse.

- "Tiger's heart wrapped in a Player's hide" was printed in a different typeface in the original, to make clear it was partially quoted from Shakespeare's *Henry VI Part 3*, in which the Duke of York says Queen Margaret has "A tiger's heart wrapped in a woman's hide."
- *"Johannes fac totum"* is Latin. It means the same as the modern "jack-of-all-trades," or someone who is good at many things, but not an expert in any.
- It ends, "in his own conceit, the only Shake-scene in the country." The pun on Shakespeare's name is obvious, and this suggests he is big-headed, too, and, in his own opinion, the best playwright.

As you can see below, Greene may not have written the *Groats-worth of Witte*, but for our purposes it doesn't matter. It shows that in the late summer of 1592, when he was 28, Shakespeare was already an actor, a playwright, and a success.

WHAT'S THE EVIDENCE?

Who Wrote the *Groatsworth of Wit*?

Robert Greene was a noted writer. He wrote successful plays, romances, and books pretending to expose con men who he had made up. He left his wife to live with another woman in a rough part of town. His death was big news—and news sells books. *Groatsworth* and two other books claimed Greene wrote them on his deathbed. Another writer, Henry Chettle, admitted preparing *Groatsworth* to be printed, and computer analysis suggests he may have written most of it. He soon apologized, saying Shakespeare was honest, upright, and a graceful writer.[4]

The idea of Greene writing three books while he was dying became a joke at the time. This 1598 pamphlet shows him writing in a **shroud**.

Dating the Plays

Scholars have to work out the most likely date by looking at lots of different evidence. Some evidence tells us the earliest possible date, other evidence the latest possible date, and yet other evidence may suggest a particular date. This evidence includes:

- When the play refers to something that happened in the real world. For example, a play that refers to the Spanish Armada must be written after 1588, when the Armada attacked England.
- When a part seems to have been written for a particular actor in Shakespeare's company, in which case it must have been written while that actor was with the company.
- When we know there was a performance, but it may not have been the first.
- If the play was performed before it was first printed or registered.

Comedies

The Two Gentlemen of Verona is a complicated story of love, jealousy, betrayal, and eventual happiness. *The Taming of the Shrew* was a rewrite of an earlier play. The earlier play still exists, so we can see the changes Shakespeare made. Improving an old play would be the type of job given to a young playwright. *The Comedy of Errors* deals with the confusions created by two sets of identical twins. One set were masters and the other were servants. It was based on a Roman play by Plautus, which Shakespeare probably studied at school. Shakespeare added the twin servants to increase the confusion.

Histories

The three plays about Henry VI were box office successes. Shakespeare was the main author, but, as was common at the time, he collaborated with other writers. Shakespeare first wrote what we call *Part 2*, then *Part 3* as a sequel, and finally *Part 1* as a prequel. New plays were often only performed three or four times, but *Part 1* was performed 15 times at the Rose between March 3 and June 19, 1592.[5] It was an enormous success. More than 30,000 people, or about 15 percent of the population of London, came to see it.[6]

Tragedies

Titus Andronicus is thought to be Shakespeare's first tragedy. *Titus Andronicus* has great moments of poetry, and of tension-relieving comedy, but it is driven by acts of brutality and revenge in a three-way quarrel between Titus and his family, the Emperor, and Tamora, queen of the Goths. Modern audiences often see similarities with the films of directors like Quentin Tarantino. Offstage during the play, Titus' daughter, Lavinia, has her hands and tongue cut off to stop her from naming Tamora's sons, Chiron and Demetrius, as her attackers. Titus has his right hand cut off (onstage), and also onstage Chiron and Demetrius have their throats cut. Offstage they are then butchered and baked in a pie, which (onstage) their mother is tricked into eating. In a final onstage frenzy, Titus kills Lavinia (out of pity) and then Tamora (for revenge), before he is killed by the Emperor, who in turn is killed by Titus' son, Lucius.

FACTS

By 1594, Shakespeare had probably written:
The Two Gentlemen of Verona
The Taming of the Shrew
Henry VI Part 2
Henry VI Part 3
Henry VI Part 1
Titus Andronicus
The Comedy of Errors

Special effects in Shakespeare's time were spectacular and gory, with real sheep's blood often used. Without modern detergents, actors had to be careful with their expensive costumes. Onstage they used pigs' bladders filled with blood or sponges soaked in blood. In the revival of *Titus* at Shakespeare's Globe in 2006, the combination of the horror of the story and the gory effects made up to 30 audience members faint or need to leave each performance!

Titus Andronicus is considered Shakespeare's bloodiest and most violent play.

Opposition to the Theater

We've seen that the Lord Mayor and the rest of the administration of London tried to stop the actors performing plays, but why? There was more than one reason.

- Some thought plays were immoral and encouraged people to sin, both because of the stories and because of the people they met at playhouses.
- Puritans and other churchmen were worried about plays as a rival attraction to religion. In a sermon, one churchman said, "Wyll not a fylthye playe wyth a blast of a Trumpette, sooner call thyther a thousande, than an houres tolling of a Bell, bring to a sermon a hundred?"[7] Performances on Sundays and holidays, considered "holy" days, were strongly opposed.
- Large numbers of people meeting together might make it easier for Roman Catholic plotters to meet and pass messages.
- The administration worried about "honesty in manners." They thought going to a play was a step on the road to immorality, drunkenness, and gambling.
- The poor would spend money they could not afford to. Business owners feared the poor might go to a play when they should be at their jobs.
- Finally, there was the threat of plague. No one knew what caused it, but people did know it was highly contagious, and two or three thousand people crushed together at a play seemed likely to spread it.

The Theaters Close

London suffered small outbreaks of plague in many summers. The outbreak of 1592–1594 was particularly serious, with one contemporary estimating that more than 10,000 died during 1593.[8] The theaters were closed, with only a few brief exceptions, from June 23, 1592, to June 1594. The playing companies toured, and struggled to survive. Shakespeare was a writer as well as an actor. How did he survive?

SHAKESPEARE'S WORLD EXPLAINED

Bubonic Plague

Death from plague was fast and painful. Victims got a headache, then tiredness, vomiting, aching joints, swellings in the groin, underarms, or neck; a fever; and sweating. Some survived, but most died in three or four days. Because Elizabethans did not know the cause, they had no useful treatments.

There were several outbreaks of the Bubonic Plague in Europe from the 14th to the 17th centuries.

How Did Writers Make Money?

The modern system of copyright and the idea of intellectual property didn't exist in the 16th century. If Shakespeare wrote a play, he sold it to the acting company, and then they owned it. As a playwright, he did not get money for each performance. He just got a lump sum at the start. In the 1590s, this was probably about £5 ($7.60). If that play was later published, he wouldn't get any more money at all. Sometimes we think the publisher just got hold of the text and printed and sold it. Other times, the acting company would sell the publisher the text to print, and they would get the money. The same system applied to books other than plays. For example, authors such as Robert Greene would write a short book and sell it to a publisher for as little as £1 ($1.50).

Greene died in poverty. It was difficult to make a good living writing pamphlets or plays, but there was another way for a writer to make money: patronage. "Respectable" books, like poetry or history books, could be dedicated to a rich and famous man or woman. Sometimes writers did this in the hope of attracting the attention of a possible patron. Other times, it was repayment because the patron had previously given the writer money, somewhere to live, or both.

What Did Shakespeare Do?

With the London theaters closed, Shakespeare had a problem. Acting and writing plays were his main ways of making money. Touring actors made less money than those in London, and the market for new plays was as dead as many plague-killed Londoners. So he turned his hand to poetry and looked for a patron.

His first long poem, *Venus and Adonis*, was published in February 1593. It was based on a classical story in Ovid's *Metamorphoses*, a book Shakespeare would have studied in school. It tells of the love of the goddess Venus for Adonis, a beautiful young man. In Ovid's story, which is 75 lines long, Adonis returns her love. In Shakespeare's version, there is much more tension as Adonis rejects her love and tries to avoid her. Shakespeare's story is longer, too—he wrote 1194 lines. It was Shakespeare's only real bestseller during his lifetime.

TO THE RIGHT
HONOVRABLE, HENRY
VVriothesley, Earle of Southhampton,
and Baron of Titchfield.

HE loue I dedicate to your Lordship is without end: whereof this Pamphlet without beginning is but a superfluous Moity. The warrant I haue of your Honourable disposition, not the worth of my vntutord Lines makes it assured of acceptance. VVhat I haue done is yours, what I haue to doe is yours, being part in all I haue, deuoted yours. VVere my worth greater, my duety would shew greater, meane time, as it is, it is bound to your Lordship; To whom I wish long life still lengthned with all happinesse.

Your Lordships in all duety.

William Shakespeare.

A 2

This is Shakespeare's dedication to the Earl of Southampton from *The Rape of Lucrece*. Only two letters written by Shakespeare are known to exist: this one and the dedication to *Venus and Adonis*. Both were meant for publication. For modern taste, it is a little over the top in the compliments it pays.

Shakespeare's second long poem, *The Rape of Lucrece* was published in May 1594. This time it is about lust, not love. Lucrece, after being attacked, kills herself. Both poems were dedicated to Henry Wriothesley (pronounced "Risley"), 3rd Earl of Southampton. Most scholars think the *Lucrece* dedication suggests, when compared to the one in *Venus*, that Shakespeare knew Southampton better, and may have received some patronage from him.

Back to the Theater

In the summer of 1594, the plague was over, and the theaters were open again. The Lord Chamberlain had a plan. He was the courtier, or adviser, responsible for Queen Elizabeth's entertainment, and he was looking for a solution to the quarrelling between the City and the Privy Council over plays in London. He came up with a new scheme. Only two companies would be allowed—his, and the Lord Admiral's. There would be no playing inside London, but his company would have the Theatre, north of the city, and the Admiral's would have the Rose, south of the Thames. The existing plays, and the best actors, seem to have been divided up as well.

Shakespeare joined the Lord Chamberlain's Men, and they started performing at the Newington Butts theater on June 3.[9] Two days later, they played *Titus Andronicus*. Soon they moved on to the Theatre. Shakespeare became a **sharer** in the company. The sharers ran the company and took the profits. Normally a sharer had to buy his share, so Shakespeare presumably had enough money to do this. At Christmas 1594, the company performed for the queen, and in March the next year, Shakespeare, as a sharer, was one of the men who collected the money when they eventually got paid.

The acting company normally took all the entrance money paid by people standing in the yard, and half of the extra money paid by those in the galleries. Out of their income, the company would buy the costumes and the plays, and pay the actors and other staff. The profits, of course, were divided among the sharers.

What Makes Shakespeare Different?

Shakespeare was known as a playwright in 1594. Soon, he was known as a master playwright. In a small section of a 666-page book, *Palladis Tamia, Wits Treasury*, entered on the Stationers' Register on September 7, 1598, Francis Meres wrote a chapter comparing the leading authors of his day to the great Roman and Greek writers:

> *the sweete wittie soule of Ovid lives in mellifluous and hony-tongued Shakespeare, witnes his Venus and Adonis, his Lucrece, his sugred Sonnets among his private friends, etc. As Plautus and Seneca are accounted the best for Comedy and Tragedy among the Latines: so Shakespeare among the English is the most excellent in both kinds for the stage; for Comedy, witnes his* Gentlemen of Verona, *his* Errors, *his* Love labors lost, *his* Love labours wonne, *his* Midsummer night dreame, & *his* Merchant of Venice: *for Tragedy his* Richard the 2. Richard the 3. Henry the 4. King John, Titus Andronicus *and his* Romeo and Juliet.... *I say that the* **Muses** *would speak with Shakespeares fine filed phrase, if they would speake English.*[1]

What made Shakespeare different from other playwrights at the time is a big part of what made him so successful so quickly. It came:

- partly from the insights he got as an actor
- partly from his skill as a writer and his profound empathy
- partly from his secure position as a sharer in his company and partial owner of a theater

Shakespeare as an Actor

Modern actors often say how well Shakespeare's text works on the stage. His experience as an actor was a great help to him as a writer. Cast lists from his time have not survived, but, when some plays were printed, they had a list of the actors, but not the parts they played. The *First Folio* lists Shakespeare as an actor in his own plays. He is listed twice in plays by Ben Jonson, as a comedian in *Every Man in His Humour* (1598), and as a tragedian in *Sejanus* (1603). He acted throughout this period, but what parts did he play? The only contemporary reference is a poem by John Davies, from 1610, which said

Here Richard III (Mark Rylance) suggests that Lady Anne (Johnny Flynn) should kill him if she will not accept him as a lover. This was an **original practices** production of *Richard III* at Shakespeare's Globe in 2012.

Shakespeare played "Kingly parts." Later tradition suggests he played the Ghost in Hamlet, but this was first recorded more than 90 years after he died.

Shakespeare the Celebrity

A Londoner's diary for March 13, 1602, tells a story about Shakespeare and Richard Burbage, a leading actor. A woman was so taken with Burbage as Richard III that she wanted to meet him after the show. Shakespeare overheard the plan, and turned up first. When Burbage arrived, he said, "Richard III is at the door." Shakespeare called down, "William the Conqueror was before Richard III." The story may or may not be true. It is the sort of celebrity gossip common today and shows us Shakespeare and Burbage were celebrities in their day.[2]

FACTS

Between 1594 and 1603 Shakespeare probably wrote:

Richard III
Love's Labor's Lost
Richard II
Romeo and Juliet
A Midsummer Night's Dream
King John
The Merchant of Venice
Henry IV Part 1
The Merry Wives of Windsor
Henry IV Part 2
Much Ado About Nothing
Henry V
Julius Caesar
As You Like It
Hamlet
Twelfth Night
Troilus and Cressida

Shakespeare as a Writer

Shakespeare's craft as a writer developed between 1594 and 1603. The characters in the plays he wrote at this time have more depth. They tell the audience about their motives and hopes in **soliloquies**. The themes become more serious. For example, in the two *Henry IV* plays, the audience is asked to think about issues like the relationship between fathers and sons, guilt, ambition, and the effects of politics on the lives of normal citizens. Shakespeare also started to use humor in a new way. The *Henry IV* plays have a comic subplot, but Shakespeare discovered a way to make these comic scenes develop the themes, and to make the characters like Falstaff full of the contradictions we find in real people.

The Sonnets

Shakespeare published a series of 154 poems called **sonnets** in 1609. He wrote at least 103 of them in the late 1590s. We know Francis Meres had read some by 1598, and two were printed in a pirate edition in 1599. This is more proof of Shakespeare's growing reputation—it was worth the publisher's risk to pirate some Shakespeare poems because they would sell well.

The sonnets are a great temptation to a biographer, because they could be looked at as autobiographical. They tell a story of the growing love between the poet and a young man, and also his love for a "dark mistress," and then his despair when he discovers the dark mistress and the young man are lovers.

Scholars have used forests of paper arguing that they have identified the other two real people in this love triangle. Candidates for the young man include the earls of Southampton and Pembroke. For the dark lady, they range from Lucy Negro, a well-known prostitute, to the poet Emilia Lanier.[3] None of these theories is completely convincing, and the sonnets may not be autobiographical at all. Shakespeare may have developed the story to make the poems more interesting. Empathy, or the ability to imagine another person's life from the inside, is one of his great skills.

The sonnets do show us an important part of Shakespeare's craft as a writer. A comparison of the two printed in the pirate edition in 1599 with the 1609 "official" versions shows small changes, which add up to a great improvement. He was a reviser. He could come back to his work and make it better. Indeed, in the plays, he rarely bothers to invent his own stories: he takes existing ones, changes them, and makes them better.

A Shakespeare Manuscript

In the *First Folio*, the actors Heminges and Condell say Shakespeare wrote fluently: "What he thought, he uttered with that easinesse, that wee have scarse received from him a blot in his papers." It is believed that this is the only surviving play manuscript in Shakespeare's handwriting. It is not a play normally thought of as written by Shakespeare. It comes from *Sir Thomas More*, a multi-author play with one Shakespeare scene, where More stops an anti-immigrant riot in London. It shows some crossing out, but his writing does seem to have flowed. The last couple of lines read:

> *That breaking out in hidious violence*
> *Would not aford you an abode on earth*

Falstaff (Roger Allam) keeps a modern audience spellbound, in *Henry IV Part 2*, at Shakespeare's Globe in 2010.

Falstaff

In the *Henry IV* plays, Sir John Falstaff is a drunkard, a liar, and a thief. He spends most of his time with criminals and prostitutes, and some of it with the future Henry V. Shakespeare makes him full of contradictions, and a compelling character at the heart of the play. But Shakespeare didn't call him Falstaff. Shakespeare originally called him Oldcastle, the name of a real knight during Henry IV's reign. Shakespeare's company performed *Henry IV Part 1* at court during Christmas 1596. It was a great success, but not with Lord Cobham, the new Lord Chamberlain. Oldcastle was one of his ancestors, and he was outraged. Shakespeare was a famous and successful actor and playwright then, and has become world famous since. But in 1596, he was nowhere near as important as Lord Cobham. Shakespeare changed the name to Falstaff, and in

FACTS

Francis Meres' list of plays by Shakespeare includes *Love's Labor's Won*. This is a mystery. It could be a different title for a surviving play—it fits *The Taming of The Shrew*—or it could have been a sequel to *Love's Labor's Lost*, which seems to end in the middle of the story. A play with this title was printed, and it is on a list of a bookseller's stock in 1603. No copy has been found yet.[4]

the epilogue to *Henry IV Part 2*, he apologized:

> our humble author will continue
> the story, with Sir John in it,
> and make you merry with fair
> Katherine of Fraunce, where (for
> anything I know) Falstaffe shall
> die of a sweat, unless already a
> be killed with your hard opinions.
> For Olde-castle dyed a martyre,
> and this is not the man.[5]

Deaths in the Family

Many scholars think Shakespeare's work gets darker in the late 1590s. In August 1596, his 11-year old son, Hamnet, died in Stratford. We don't know why he died, nor whether Shakespeare was in Stratford or in London at the time. We may see his grief in the lines he wrote that year in *King John*, as Lady Constance mourns her son: "Grief fills the room up of my absent child: | Lies in his bed, walks up and down with me."[6] But it can be dangerous for a biographer to use the plays in this way. These lines come in a passage where Constance is criticized for showing too much grief.

Less unexpectedly, Shakespeare's father, John, died in his seventies in September 1601.

Myth Shakespeare Wrote Alone

More than 50 percent of Elizabethan and **Jacobean** plays were collaborations between two or more playwrights. Shakespeare mainly wrote alone, but he also collaborated with other writers. An early collaboration is *Henry VI Part 1* (collaborator unknown). At the end of his career, he wrote with John Fletcher (who succeeded him as the company's playwright). Together they wrote three plays: *Henry VIII*, *The Two Noble Kinsmen*, and *Cardenio*. Only *Henry VIII* is in the *First Folio*, and the text of *Cardenio* has not survived. Scholars think he also worked with other writers in *Timon of Athens*, *All's Well That Ends Well*, and *Pericles*. There are also plays such as *Sir Thomas More* and *Edward III*, where Shakespeare wrote a scene or two in a multi-author play.[7]

Myth Queen Elizabeth and *Merry Wives of Windsor*

There is a myth that Queen Elizabeth enjoyed Falstaff so much that she demanded a new play where Falstaff is in love (*Merry Wives of Windsor*). She gave Shakespeare two weeks to get it ready, so she could see it. The truth is that this tale was first printed in 1702, over 100 years later, and it was linked to a new performance of the play. It is unlikely to be true.

Problems with Playhouses

The Lord Chamberlain's Men were playing in the Theatre in late 1596. James Burbage owned it, and his son Richard was the star actor in the company. However, James only leased the land, and the **lease** ended on March 25, 1597. James died early in 1597, and the lease passed to his son Cuthbert. The landlord, Giles Allen, wanted the land back, and would not renew the lease. The company played on at the Theatre for a few months, then moved to the nearby Curtain.[8]

Both the Theatre and the Curtain were old playhouses, smaller than the newer Rose and Swan theaters, which were south of the river on Bankside. James Burbage had planned to move the company to a new indoor playhouse, in what had been part of the Blackfriars monastery, which he bought and fitted out. This plan failed because the other residents of the Blackfriars got the Privy Council to ban the planned theater.

This photo shows the building of the modern Globe, which opened on Bankside in 1997. It is a reconstruction of the original theater made as accurately as possible. The framework of structural timbers take the weight of the structure, and the gaps are then filled in with lath and plaster, and doors and windows. See page 43 for a look at the finished theater.

Both the Burbage brothers and the Lord Chamberlain's Men were in trouble. Cuthbert and Richard Burbage had little or no money— James had spent it all on the failed Blackfriars plan. With the company at the Curtain, the Burbages weren't getting the theater owner's share of the takings. The Curtain was an old and small theater, which was bad for the company, too. The solution was appropriately dramatic. The Burbages would raise some money, take down the Theatre building, and use its timbers to make a new and better theater on Bankside.

Building the Globe

First, they had to raise the money. The system of running the Lord Chamberlain's Men by sharers was working, so they extended it to the ownership of the new theater. The Burbages created ten shares, kept five, and offered one each to Shakespeare and four other actors. These shareowners were called **housekeepers**.

WHAT'S THE EVIDENCE?

How Do We Know About Taking the Theatre Down?

No financial records of the Lord Chamberlain's Men survive, nor do any of the business papers of the Burbages. We only know this story because the landlord, Giles Allen, sued the Burbages and the builder for damages and the return of the timbers. Some of the statements from both sides in the court case survive, but of course, each side tells their own version of the story. For example, Allen said the Burbages and their men had "ryotouslye assemble...armed with divers and many unlawfull and offensive weapons."[9] It was in his interest to make things sound as bad as possible.

Theater on the Move

The Theatre lease that Burbage had with Allen said Burbage owned, and could take down, anything he built on the land—and he had built the Theatre. So on December 28, during a snowy night, the Burbages, with a gang of actors, builders, and some hired muscle, turned up and started taking down the Theatre. It would have taken several days. Timber-framed buildings work a bit like ready-to-assemble furniture. The carpenter made the framework in his yard, then took it apart, transported to the site, and re-built it. You can see the frame clearly in the photo of the reconstructed Globe. Taking the structural timbers down meant they could be reused in a different building. Builders in the 16th century often did this, and this time they used the timbers to build the Globe Theatre, which opened in 1599.

Businessman

Shakespeare was now a businessman as well as an actor and a playwright. He was part-owner of the Globe, London's newest, largest, and grandest theater. It was also a theater built by actors for actors. Actors made all the decisions about how big the stage should be and what the sightlines would be. A German tourist described a visit to the Globe on September 21, 1599:

> After dinner, about two o'clock, I went with my companions over the water, and in the thatched [play]house, we saw the tragedy of the first Emperor Julius Caesar, very well acted, with at least 15 characters. At the end of the play, they danced together admirably and exceedingly gracefully, according to their custom, two in each group dressed in men's and two in women's clothes.[10]

He had been to Shakespeare's *Julius Caesar*. Shakespeare had been paid for writing the play, he got a share of the acting company's profits from the performance, and he got a share of the theater owner's profits, too. This means two things. First, Shakespeare the businessman was starting to make money— and in the next chapter we'll look at what he did with it. Second, it also means that Shakespeare the writer had more freedom. He didn't have to keep quickly writing more plays to make a living. He could afford to take more time, and more care, than other playwrights.

Treason!

The last years of Elizabeth's reign were difficult. Harvests were bad, food was expensive, and some people starved. Elizabeth had no children, and discussion about who should be the next monarch was forbidden. In 1601, the Earl of Essex, once Elizabeth's **favorite**, but now under house arrest, planned a rebellion. His supporters included the Earl of Southampton, who earlier was probably Shakespeare's patron. Some of the rebels approached the Lord Chamberlain's Men and asked them to perform Shakespeare's *Richard II* at the Globe on February 7. In the play, Richard is forced to **abdicate**, and Henry IV takes the throne. The plotters hoped it would put Londoners in the mood for a revolt. They were wrong, and Essex's rebellion the next day was easily squashed.

Rebuilding the Globe

Shakespeare's Globe, as it is called, was the idea of Sam Wanamaker, an American actor and director. He spent more than 20 years raising the money but died before it was finished. Scholars played a key part, collecting all the possible evidence about the size and shape of the original Globe theater. However, this was very inconclusive. They had to make many inferences, just as we do in looking at Shakespeare's life,

and the resulting building is as accurate as it can be, and must be very like the original.

The Lord Chamberlain's Men were in trouble. The government didn't believe in coincidences and wanted an explanation for the performance of *Richard II*. It summoned one of the sharers to explain. A group of men, he said, wanted to see the play, and asked them to put it on that Saturday. The actors didn't like the idea, saying it was an old play and they would get a poor crowd. The men offered them £2 ($3) to do it, on top of the money they took at the box office. They weren't traitors, just businessmen who took a good deal. They were forgiven, and played for the queen the night before Essex's execution.[11]

Shakespeare had survived a difficult moment. When the Queen died, in 1603, he was a successful man, but what would happen next?

FACTS

Christmas 1596 *Henry IV Part 1* performed at court.
September 7, 1598 Francis Meres praises Shakespeare's poems and plays.
1599 Two Shakespeare sonnets are printed in a pirate edition.
Summer 1599 The Globe Theatre opens with Shakespeare as a shareholder.

Was Shakespeare Rich?

People have been interested in whether Shakespeare was rich, since soon after he died. Forty-five years later, John Ward, then vicar of Stratford, wrote Shakespeare had "an allowance so large hee spent att the Rate of £1000 [$1,500] a year as I have heard".[1] Spending that much each year would mean he was very wealthy. But is this true or a myth? We might say great show business entrepreneurs today, such as Andrew Lloyd Webber, are rich, but Shakespeare lived in a very **hierarchical** society. To make sense of this question in his world, we have to answer two questions: was he moving upwards in the class system, and did he have a lot of money?

William Shakespeare, Gentleman

We've seen that Shakespeare was the son of a small-town trader, and that his father, John, grew in prosperity and then hit hard times. John had approached the College of Arms about being recognized as a gentleman, but dropped the scheme when his business was in trouble.

What did it mean to be a gentleman? The answer is simple: it meant a step up the social hierarchy. A gentleman had a coat of arms and higher status. Even in 1597, it was looking back to medieval times, where bearing arms meant both having a coat of arms and being able to raise and equip soldiers to fight for the monarch.

SHAKESPEARE'S WORLD EXPLAINED

The College of Arms

The College of Arms still exists. As in Shakespeare's day, it grants coats of arms. The College is a group of officials called heralds. Heralds have medieval titles, such as "Garter King of Arms", "Portcullis Pursuivant", and "York Herald." The College is still on the site Shakespeare went to near St. Paul's Cathedral. The building Shakespeare visited burned down in the Great Fire of London (1666), and was rebuilt. The heralds saved all the records, and they include the original notes for the Shakespeare application.

In 1596, the Shakespeares went back to the Garter King of Arms, a herald at the College of Arms. The application was in John's name. It had to be, as he was the "head" of the family. But scholars assume it was handled by William—a successful man based in London. If it was William, then he was successful in this, too. The Shakespeares got their coat of arms, and the status of gentlemen. William was proud. In all legal documents after the grant, he signs himself "William Shakespeare, gentleman."[2]

However, a problem arose in 1602. Another herald complained the Garter King of Arms had been granting coats of arms to inappropriate people, and one of his examples was "Shakespear the Player."[3] Calling Shakespeare a player (actor) was a deliberate attempt to make him sound unworthy. Players were often listed with vagabonds and **sturdy beggars** in Elizabethan law. However, the grant of arms to the Shakespeares was upheld. One thing we do learn from the complaint is it still made sense to call Shakespeare an actor in 1602.

The Shakespeare coat of arms is on the monument in the church in Stratford put up by William Shakespeare's family immediately after his death. Putting it on his monument suggests they were proud to have been granted a coat of arms.

We have the answer to the first part of our enquiry. Shakespeare was rising up the social scale.

This is the only picture of New Place. George Vertue visited Stratford in 1737, over 100 years after Shakespeare died. He made this sketch later, from memory.

Man of Property

We know Shakespeare was living in London in 1597, just inside the old city wall, a short walk from the Theatre and the Curtain playhouses. He was either renting a house or living as a lodger in somebody else's. By 1599, he had moved south of the river, near the Globe. Later, in the early 1600s, he was living as a lodger in a house back north of the river in Silver Street. But when he wanted to buy a house, and to invest in property, he didn't think about London—he thought about Stratford.

We assume, but we don't know, that Anne and their children always lived with William's parents in the family home in Stratford. When William decided to buy a house in 1597, it was in Stratford. The deeds say he paid £60 ($90) for New Place, which was the second largest house in the town. He probably paid much more. People kept the price down in official documents to keep their tax bills low, and then made a secret extra payment. This was the house a successful man would buy, and Shakespeare probably spent more money improving it. He sold a load of stone to the Council in 1598, which we assume was left over from building work.

New Place had extensive gardens, and Shakespeare enlarged them, buying land at the end of his garden, and knocking down a cottage. It had two gardens, two barns, and two orchards. The house itself was large. A survey 47 years after Shakespeare died said it had 10 fireplaces, which means it had more than 10 rooms. The site of the house and gardens can still be seen in Stratford.

In England, in Shakespeare's time and for hundreds of years after, if you made money from "trade," you then invested it in land. This provided a steady stream of income, and it is exactly what Shakespeare did.

In 1602, he bought 127 acres (51 hectares) of land, plus grazing rights on common land for £320 ($490). In the English Midlands in 2013, farmable land sold for around £7,500 ($11,500) an acre. At today's prices Shakespare's land would cost more than £1 million ($1.5 million).[4] This doesn't mean Shakespeare became a farmer. He probably rented out the land. Living on income from rent is how a gentleman was expected to live.

Shakespeare's property dealings show he was a wealthy man and one who was investing his money carefully and conventionally.

SHAKESPEARE'S WORLD EXPLAINED

Money Then and Now

In the 400-plus years since Shakespeare bought New Place, the value British people give to property has changed. Part of the reason is supply and demand. In 1600, the population of England was perhaps 4 million, whereas it was nearly 53 million in 2011. There was plenty of space in 1600, even in towns. Now 10 times as many people fit in the same area. Today, New Place might cost £1.75 million ($2.7 million).

Businessman and Investor

Some people have accused Shakespeare of being a tax dodger, a hoarder, and a **usurer**. They say that a great poet and playwright would be too sensitive to behave in such a way. The records do show us that Shakespeare was careful with money, and was concerned to make sure his family wasn't hit by poverty, as it was when he was a boy. But was he as greedy about money and uncaring about people as has been suggested?

Shakespeare paid his taxes late two times, not paying his 1597 and 1598 taxes until 1601.[5] The records about nonpayment of tax also tell us where he was living in those years. These aren't the only years when tax records survive, and since these are the only years he is listed as not paying, he probably usually paid on time. As for the charge of tax-dodger, the answer is "not very guilty."

Shakespeare is sometimes accused of being a hoarder and a usurer. For these accusations, the verdict is "a bit guilty."[6] Today, being a "hoarder" is what we might call being a "speculator." When there was a shortage of goods, such as grain and malt, hoarders bought, waited for the price to go up, and then sold at a high profit. In 1598, to stop people hoarding, the government ordered a census of all holdings of grain and malt. Shakespeare had 80 bushels of malt in his barn. Some would have been for the household's own brewing. We do know he later sold malt, so he may have been doing some speculating, but not on a large scale. He only had the third largest holding in his own street. We also know he sold malt on credit in 1604 and lent money to neighbors and business partners. He twice sued for the nonpayment of debts owed to him.

Shakespeare's biggest investment was in tithes. A tithe was a charge of a tenth of the value of income—in this case, the income from farming land. The church was financed by the collection of tithes. To raise money, it sold the right to collect some tithes around Stratford for 92 years. Shakespeare bought into the last 31 years of this lease for £440 ($670). The tithes gave him a profit of £60 ($90) a year.[7] The investment would take 8 years to get back its cost, and would then make profits for 23 years, eventually earning a total profit of £1,420 ($2,200), or 323 percent. This is another cautious investment, like land. If Shakespeare was serious about being a moneylender, he could have earned more by lending money at a high interest rate than by buying the tithes.

SHAKESPEARE'S WORLD EXPLAINED

Tax Records

Taxes were based on the value of your possessions. The valuations were not very accurate. Richard Burbage, star actor and fellow shareholder in the Globe and the Lord Chamberlain's Men, had his goods valued at £3 ($4.50) in the same assessment in which Shakespeare's were valued at £5 ($7.60).

A Cautious Investor

These transactions show us Shakespeare took good care of his money. He was a rich man, with a rich man's house and investments. But he wasn't fabulously wealthy, like a great aristocrat. He was transferring the money he made from the theater to property, land, and tithes. The theater might not be safe in the long term. Plague could shut theaters for a year or two, or the Puritans could get them closed for good. Shakespeare wasn't a gambler; he chose safe and respectable investments, acting like a typical country gentleman. And he had become a gentleman, if not a typical one.

At the start of this chapter, we saw a later vicar of Stratford estimate Shakespeare spent £1,000 ($1,500) a year. We can now see that this is myth, not reality. The income he needed to make these investments was probably only £300–£400 ($450–$600) a year.

FACTS

November 15, 1597 Shakespeare is listed as not having paid his taxes in St. Helen's parish, London.

February 4, 1598 At a time of malt and grain shortage, he is listed as having 80 bushels of malt in Stratford.

October 1, 1598 He is listed as not having paid his next tax bill in St. Helen's parish.

October 25, 1598 After this date, he probably lent Richard Quiney £30.

1599 A list of unpaid taxes for St. Helen's parish says he has moved to Bankside.

1601 Shakespeare's back taxes are probably paid.

1604 He sold Philip Rogers, an apothecary in Stratford, 20 bushels of malt on credit.

July 24, 1605 Shakespeare buys interest in tithes.

August 17, 1608 He sues Richard Addenbroke of Stratford for a debt of £6 ($9) plus damages.

The King's Man

Shakespeare's company performed before Queen Elizabeth for the last time on February 2, 1603. By this point, she was old and sick. In March, she fell ill, refused to go to bed, and sat in a chair day and night. She refused food, and refused to be treated by her doctors. Elizabeth died on March 24. Until the last day of her life, she refused to say who should rule after her death. But Sir Robert Cecil said that on the last day she whispered to him that it should be her cousin, James VI of Scotland.

James was 37 when he became James I of England. He was a successful king of Scotland and a well-read and intelligent man. On the other hand, he had some odd characteristics. He usually wore heavily padded **doublets** because he was scared of being stabbed, his tongue was said to be too big for his mouth, and he sometimes got very drunk at public feasts. As King of Scotland, he had always been short of money, and England seemed a very rich country to him. He was generous, giving lavish gifts to his favorites.

His generosity continued. Ten days after reaching London, he issued an order for the Lord Chamberlain's Men to become his own troupe of players—the King's Men. A **royal patent** quickly followed:

> *lawrence ffletcher, William Shakespeare, Richard Burbage, Augustine Phillippes, John Heminges, Henrie Condell, [three others] and the rest of theire Assosiates freely to use and exercise the Arte and faculty of playinge Comedies Tragedies histories Enterludes moralls pastoralls Stage plaies and suche others like as theie have alreadie studied or hereafter shall use or studie aswell for the recreation of our lovinge Subjectes as for our Solace and pleasure when wee shall thincke good to see them duringe our pleasure. And ... to shewe and exercise publiquely to theire best Commoditie when the infection of the plague shall decrease aswell within their nowe usual howse called the Globe within our County of Surrey as also within anie towne halls or Moute halls or other conveniente places within the liberties and freedome of anie Cittie universittie towne or Boroughe whatsoever within our said Realmes and dominions.*[1]

Did It Make Any Difference?

This is a powerful document. It gives the company the king's patronage, and when they needed to tour, they could say that the king wanted them to be able to play in any town, borough, or university—a powerful encouragement to local councils not to send them away.

We can learn from it as well. There were three main acting companies in London in 1603. Shakespeare's must have been the most successful, because they got the King's patronage. The other companies became the Queen's Men and the Prince's Men.

King James VI and I (c. 1606) was painted about three years after he became King of England.

In the last 10 years of Elizabeth's reign, Shakespeare's company played at court 32 times, an average of just over three times a year. In the first 10 years of James' reign, the company played at court 138 times, an average of just under 14 times a year. So as the King's Men, and with a king who wanted to see more plays, they played at court much more often.

They didn't just act in plays for the king. The sharers had the rank of "Grooms of the Chamber," and as such, they were issued with 4½ yards of red cloth to make their official clothes. They needed them to wear when they took part in the King's coronation procession in March 1604.[2] They probably also wore them when they were used as special attendants to wait on the Spanish ambassador, who was in England in August that year to sign a peace treaty. Presumably they were chosen because they were imposing-looking men, who knew how to behave—and act. Shakespeare had come a long way—from a glover's shop in Stratford to being a servant of the king.

Royal Records

The King's Men kept careful records, but they have not all survived. The royal court, however, kept records that have survived, so more is known about performances at court than about those at the Globe. Opposite is a page from the accounts of the Revels Office, which arranged for plays to be seen by the king and the court. It is divided into three columns. The first column lists the company of actors, the "plaiers." The middle column gives the date and the play. The third column is headed "the poets," the term used for playwrights. The third entry from the bottom reads:

By his Ma^{tis}   *On Shrousunday A play of the*   *Shaxberd*
plaiers: -   *Marthant of Venis*

His Majesty's Players means the King's Men. The day is **Shrove** Sunday, and the play *The Merchant of Venice*. Shaxberd is one of the more unusual spellings of Shakespeare. Shrovetide was a three-day festival before the beginning of Lent, with plays each day. On Shrove Tuesday (two days later), we have *The Martchant of Venis Againe Commanded By the Kings Matie*. King James enjoyed the play so much, he insisted on a second performance. Almost certainly, another play already would have been booked for that day, perhaps from another company.

Records like these can be hard to read. The odd spelling may show the clerk spoke with a Scots accent, but it isn't only the spelling that is different. Handwriting has changed since 1605, too. Look at the third entry from the bottom and compare it with the transcript above.

◆ s can be written as it is now, or as a long stroke with a tail below the line (*Srousunday*)
◆ t may not be crossed, and h has a curled tail below the line and e can look like a modern r (*the*)
◆ V can look like u (*Venis*)
◆ when n m i are written together you just get a series of downstrokes, joined at the top. These are called minims (*Venis*).

Can you find another play that could be by Shakespeare? (A clue: it doesn't have *Shaxberd* in the poet column.)

The plaiers	On Twelfe Night	The poets

The plaiers On Twelfe Night By the Quens matis Maske of Moures and of Eleven Ladies to keep Company with the matis in a maske in great somes of Devised with excellent musike

By his ma^{tis} plaiers: On the 7 of January was played the play of Henry the fift

By his ma^{tis} plaiers: The 8 of January A play Cauled Every on out of his Umor

By his ma^{tis} plaiers: On Candelmas night A playe Every one In his Umor

The Sunday ffollowing A playe probited And dissplayed

By his ma^{tis} plaiers: On Shrousunday A play of the Marthant of Veins — Shaxberd

By his ma^{tis} plaiers: On Shroumonday A Tragide of the Spanishe Maz

By his ma^{tis} plaiers: On Shroutusday A play Cauled The Marchant of Venis Againe Comanded By the Kings Matie — Shaxberd

53

A Lodger in Silver Street

In 1604, in London, Shakespeare lived in the house of the Mountjoys in Silver Street, north of the river, just inside London's old city walls. They were French Protestant refugees, working in the fashion industry, making expensive women's hats called tires. It was a quiet area of London, north of the bustle of Cheapside, the main shopping street, and west of Wood Street, a main road out of the city through Cripplegate. To walk to the Globe would take just over half an hour, crossing the river at London Bridge.

We know Shakespeare lived with the Mountjoys, because some events in 1604 finished up as a court case in 1612. Shakespeare testified in the case, and his testimony, written down by the clerk, is the only record we have of anything he said. The court case concerns the marriage of Stephen Belott, the Mountjoys' former apprentice (who lived with and worked for them) and Mary, their only child. There was talk of a marriage, but nothing was settled. Shakespeare was asked by Mrs. Mountjoy to "move and perswade" Belott to marry Mary, and he did "move and perswade [him] thereunto."

The issue in court was Mary's dowry. Belott claimed he was promised £60 ($90), and £200 ($300) in Mountjoy's will. Asked by another witness, earlier in the quarrel, Shakespeare said it was "ffyftye poundes in money and Certain Househould stuffe," but when it came to court he changed his mind. By then he "rememberithe not, nor knoweth" about the £200 ($300).[3]

What should we make of this? Was Shakespeare getting old and forgetful? He was 40 in 1604, and 48 when he testified in court. Did he change his story, or was the other witness making a false claim? As so often, even when we have evidence, we have more questions than answers.

Another man involved in the court case was George Wilkins. Wilkins was an shady character who had been convicted of violent acts. He had a short career as a writer, and he and Shakespeare collaborated on *Pericles* in 1607 or 1608.

Part of a map of London, probably made in the 1560s. The Mountjoy's house is marked in red, on the corner of Muggle Street (blue) and Silver Street (yellow). John Heminges, friend and colleague of Shakespeare in the King's Men, and an editor of the First Folio, lived nearby in Addle Street (green).

| Muggle Street | Silver Street |
| The Mountjoy's house | Addle Street |

Playing Indoors

In 1596, when he was worried about the lease of the Theatre, James Burbage invested in one of the largest indoor spaces in the whole of London, the Parliament Chamber, which had been part of the old Blackfriars monastery. It was called this because Parliament had met there a number of times, most recently in 1523. He converted it into an indoor theater, but his plans alarmed his new neighbors, who got the Privy Council to ban its use as a professional theater. James died in 1597, and the conversion costs almost bankrupted his sons, Richard and Cuthbert. In 1600, the Burbage brothers leased the Blackfriars theater to Henry Evans, who set up a children's company to act there. After producing a number of politically controversial plays, the children's company was banned by order of King James. In 1608, Evans gave the lease back to Richard Burbage.

The Blackfriars Theatre

Now that the company was the *King's* Men, it had enough powerful support to be able to use its indoor theatre. The system of shareholders owning the Globe was working well, and the Burbages extended it to the Blackfriars. Shakespeare got a one-seventh share, which, after another housekeeper died, became a one-sixth share. But what was their "new" theater like?

- It was much smaller than the Globe. From the back wall of the stage to the end of the **auditorium** was 66 feet (20 m), and it can have been no more than 46 feet (14 m) wide.
- Unlike the Globe, there were no stage pillars, because the whole building had a roof.
- The stage was smaller than the Globe, but, like the Globe, it did have two side doors plus a central door, or **discovery space**, in the back wall. There was a **stage trap** halfway between the back wall and the front of the stage.
- Like the Globe, **galleries** for the audience to sit in ran round the auditorium, and now they ran along the side of the stage, as you can see in the photo. Fashionable young men, known as gallants, could choose to sit on stools on the stage itself.
- The most significant difference was the lighting. Performances started about 2:00 p.m. and finished about 5:00 p.m. There were windows, but 5:00 p.m. in a London winter is dark, and they used hundreds of candles.

This performance took place in a modern reconstruction of the Blackfriars Playhouse at the American Shakespeare Center, Staunton, Virginia.

A New Plan—and More Profit

From 1609, the King's Men had a new plan: perform at the Globe in the summer and the Blackfriars in the winter. They normally switched over in May and October. The Blackfriars only held about 500 people, while the Globe held 3,000; but the prices and profits were higher indoors. Blackfriars had no standing. The cheapest seats were in the galleries. More expensive seats were the benches in the pit, which was similar to the yard, and stools on the stage. The most costly seats were boxes in the galleries. We know the company's income from just 10 performances at the Globe and Blackfriars, and the average profit was over double per performance at Blackfriars.

This new plan occurred at the end of Shakespeare's career, and he only wrote six plays in which he could have been thinking about performing in the new theater. However, the text for some of his earlier plays was revised for the Blackfriars, as we will see when we look at *Macbeth*.

Did Shakespeare's Writing Develop?

Shakespeare's plays didn't change overnight when Elizabeth died. The most significant change in his later writing, which started before 1603, is that he tells us less about the motives of major characters. This adds a depth and complexity to the plays. For example, in *King Lear*, the play starts with a "love test": the king will divide his kingdom between his three daughters, and each must tell him how much she loves him. Shakespeare took the story from an earlier play, in which this is a way to trick the youngest, Cordelia, into marrying the man her father prefers. Shakespeare's Lear doesn't have this motive, and the audience have to work out why for themselves. This makes Lear seem more, not less, human, because in our lives few people act with obvious motives.[4]

FACTS

Between 1603 and 1610 Shakespeare probably wrote:

Measure for Measure
Othello
*All's Well That
    Ends Well*
Timon of Athens (with
    Thomas Middleton)
King Lear
Macbeth
Antony and Cleopatra
Pericles (with
    George Wilkins)
Coriolanus
The Winter's Tale
Cymbeline

In this scene from the Shakespeare's Globe 2008 production of *King Lear*, Cordelia (Jodie McNee) fails her father's "love test." She says she loves Lear (David Calder), but when she marries, she will love her husband as much.

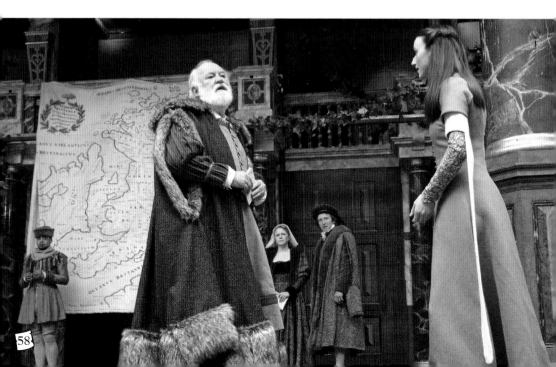

No single theme unites Shakespeare's plays from 1603, when James became king, to 1610. Some scholars suggest he got ideas and insights from the people he met during these years:

- The Mountjoys and the problems of being an immigrant may have helped when writing *Othello*, who was a black immigrant in Venice.
- George Wilkins, and the seedy world he lived in, may have supplied some ideas for *Measure for Measure*.
- Stephen Belott and Mary Mountjoy may have given him some insights into the problems of a couple where the woman was more in love than the man, which is the central storyline in *All's Well That Ends Well*.

Other scholars suggest he was more concerned with writing plays to please the king:

- *King Lear* shows the dangers of a divided kingdom. (James tried to unite England and Scotland.)
- *Measure for Measure* is about how a ruler should behave.
- *Macbeth* shows one of King James' ancestors as a hero.

There is some truth in both these views, but not enough. Shakespeare was an artist writing about what interested him. He was also a businessman who wrote to please an audience—both in the theaters and at court. He picked up ideas from books and from the world around him. Shakespeare's great skill is to have pleased an audience *and* written plays that tackle serious and universal themes. He did this while making them interesting, with various ideas and insights he picked up from all over his world.

FACTS

February 2, 1603 *A Midsummer Night's Dream* is performed at court.
May 17, 1603 James I becomes Shakespeare's company's patron. The company is known as the King's Men.
1604 Shakespeare is living on Silver Street in London.
March 15, 1604 Shakespeare and other King's Men players take part in James' coronation procession.
August 1604 Shakespeare and other King's Men players act as attendants to the Spanish Ambassador.
November 1, 1604–February 12, 1605 *Othello*, *Measure for Measure*, *Love's Labour's Lost*, *Henry V*, and *The Merchant of Venice* (twice) are performed at court.
December 26, 1606 *King Lear* is performed at court.
1608 Shakespeare becomes a housekeeper, or shareholder, in the Blackfriars Playhouse.
September 9, 1608 Shakespeare's mother, Mary, is buried in Stratford.

Did Shakespeare Retire?

There aren't many questions about Shakespeare that have a simple answer, and the question of whether he retired is no different. Let's take a look at his writing and his life in London and Stratford to get to our answer.

Writing Plays

We have seen Shakespeare was slowing down. In the eight years from 1603 to 1610, he only produced 11 plays. This pattern continues. His 47th birthday was in April 1611, and he only wrote four plays in his remaining five years of life. What is more, three of these plays were collaborations with John Fletcher, who seems to have replaced him as the King's Men's resident playwright.

Some scholars suggest that *The Tempest*, the only one of the last four plays he wrote on his own, shows Shakepeare was thinking about retirement. The central character, Prospero, is a magician who has:

> be-dimmed
> *The noontide sun, called forth the mutinous winds,*

and

> *Graves at my command*
> *Have waked their sleepers, oped, and let 'em forth*
> *By my so potent art. But this rough magic*
> *I here abjure* [give up].[1]

It is very tempting to see this as Shakespeare describing his own life. As a great playwright, he had made day feel like night; he *had* called forth storms and battles, and he *had* raised the dead, from Anthony and Cleopatra to Henry VII. "Rough magic" would be a great description for his work. But we should probably resist the temptation to read it as autobiography. Shakespeare went on after *The Tempest* to make the dead live again in *Henry VIII*, lovers fall madly in love in *Two Noble Kinsmen*, and we don't know what kind of magic in *Cardenio*, because the text is lost.

We can say the later plays tend to concentrate on the problems familiar to older people, but even so, in *The Two Noble Kinsmen*, the last play he wrote, he is again concerned with the erratic behavior of young lovers.

Collaborators

John Fletcher was an up-and-coming playwright. He may have caught Shakespeare's attention by writing a sequel to *The Taming of the Shrew*, called *The Woman's Prize*.[2] In the original, set in Padua, Italy, Petruchio "tames" his violent and angry wife. In the sequel, after the death of his wife, Petruchio moves to London, where his attempts to change the behavior of his new wife, a Londoner, fail miserably. She tames *him*. We can't know whether this was a deliberate ploy to interest Shakespeare or not. If it was, it worked. In 1613–1614, they wrote three plays together.

Shakespeare was also collaborating with Robert Johnson, a royal **lutenist** and composer. Johnson wrote songs for a number of King's Men plays, including Shakespeare's *Cymbeline*, *The Winter's Tale*, *The Tempest*, and *Cardenio*. This fits with the greater importance of music in plays at the Blackfriars playhouse, as these are probably all of the plays Shakespeare wrote after the company started using it.

It wasn't a complete retirement from writing, at least until after 1614, but it might have been semi-retirement, with more time spent in Stratford.

Here, Prospero (Roger Allam) is just about to break his staff and give up magic at the Shakespeare Globe 2013.

The Tempest Was Shakespeare's Last Play

Myth

This is an easy one to disprove. *The Tempest* was performed at the royal court on November 1, 1611. *Henry VIII* was first performed at the Globe in June 1613.

FACTS

Between 1611 and 1616, Shakespeare probably wrote:
The Tempest
Henry VIII (with John Fletcher)
Cardenio (with John Fletcher, lost)
The Two Noble Kinsmen (with John Fletcher)

Shakespeare's Final London Years

Plague hit London with unusual force in August 1608. The Council closed the theaters, and they did not reopen until late 1609 or early 1610. We don't know where Shakespeare spent this time, but it seems reasonable to infer he spent it out of London. During the closure, the King's Men did quite a bit of touring—we know they were in the Midlands, East Anglia, Oxford, and Kent. Shakespeare may have gone with the company on the tours, or he may have spent the time in Stratford. We can be reasonably certain he gave up acting before 1613, and perhaps before 1610.[3]

We know Shakespeare was in London for the Belott Mountjoy court case in May 1612, and he was there in March 1613, because he bought another property. This one was the gatehouse to the old Blackfriars monastery, very close to the Blackfriars Playhouse, and also close to the river where he could get a **wherry** to take him across to the Globe. There are a few odd things about this house purchase. The contract price was £140 ($213), but he probably would have paid more. He didn't have all the money, and had to borrow £60 ($90). Also, he bought the house with three other men as trustees, given a joint responsibility to manage the property. It is tempting to see this as Shakespeare buying a perfectly placed London home, but he rented it out, so it seems to have been another investment.

There is no doubt about the next event. On June 29, 1613, during a performance of Shakespeare's new play, *Henry VIII*, the Globe burned down. In a letter written to his nephew, Sir Henry Wotton described what happened:

> certain chambers [cannon fired from an attic window in the tiring house] being shot off at his [Henry VIII's] entry, some of the paper ... wherewith one of them was stopped, did light on the thatch, where ... their eyes more attentive to the show, it kindled inwardly, and ran round ... consuming within less than an hour the whole house to the very grounds. This was the fatal period of that virtuous fabric, wherein yet nothing did perish, but wood and straw, and a very few forsaken cloaks; only one man had his breeches set on fire, that would perhaps have broiled him, if he had not by the benefit of a provident wit put it out with bottle ale.[4]

The fire was such major news that reports were printed describing it. They mention Burbage, Heminges, and Condell, but not Shakespeare. If he was there, he surely was famous enough to be mentioned, so we may infer he was not there, which suggests he had stopped acting by 1613.

The King's Men decided to rebuild the Globe, and each shareholder had to contribute £50–£60 ($75–$90) to the rebuilding costs. We know Shakespeare was short of cash in March, when he needed a mortgage to buy the Blackfriars gatehouse. This may be why he took on the small job of designing a tournament shield and motto for the Earl of Rutland, for a small fee, paid at the end of the month. Perhaps this is the moment he chose to sell his share in the Globe? As so often, there is no evidence.

Shakespeare certainly didn't stop visiting London. In November 1614, Thomas Greene wrote, "My cosen Shakespeare commying yesterday to towne I went to see him howe he did."[5] He was almost certainly in London in May 1615 for a court case about the Gatehouse property.

The most likely interpretation of this evidence is that Shakespeare hadn't cut all his connections to London, but he may well have spent less time there. He was still an investor and a man of the theater, but probably a semiretired one.

The rebuilt Globe theater had a tiled roof to prevent further fires. In 1647, the engraver mixed up the labels—the Globe is labelled *Beere Bayting* and the arena for Bear Baiting is labelled *The Globe*. The building to the left of the Globe is the tap house, or bar, where the bottle of beer used on the burning breeches probably came from (see page 62).

Family Matters

Shakespeare's elder daughter, Susanna, married on June 5, 1607. Her husband, John Hall, was a successful doctor. Their daughter, Elizabeth, baptized on February 21, 1608, was Shakespeare's first grandchild, the only one born while he was alive. William's two surviving brothers died in February 1612 and February 1613. This left William and his sister, Joan Hart, as the only surviving siblings.

Shakespeare had a bad summer in 1613. On June 29, the Globe burnt down. On July 15, the trouble was in Stratford. Susanna sued a local man, John Lane, for **slander**. Lane had accused her of being unfaithful to Dr. Hall. He offered no defense, and Susanna won her case. Next year, on July 9, a "suddaine and terrible Fire" destroyed 54 houses in Stratford as well as barns and stables, but all Shakespeare's property survived.[6]

The Welcome Enclosure

In September 1614, three large landowners planned to enclose land around the small village of Welcome, where Shakespeare owned half the tithes. The villagers, supported by the Stratford Council, opposed the plan. Both sides wanted Shakespeare's support. He was an influential man in the town. In January 1615, work on boundary ditches started. Two councilors bought land in the fields, then because they were small landowners with rights, started to fill in the ditches. The enclosers' men stopped them and beat them. The next day, women and children from Stratford and the villages went out to fill the ditches. The enclosers couldn't face attacking them, so the scheme failed.

But what did Shakespeare do? On October 28, 1614, he made a private deal with the enclosers. If the value of his tithes fell because of the enclosures, they would compensate him. With his own finances secure, he did not support either side in public. At the height of the crisis, on December 23, the Stratford Council wrote again, asking for his support. He seems to have done nothing.

What does this tell us about Shakespeare? He wasn't a community leader looking after the interests of the poor, and he wasn't a supporter of enclosure as a necessary change in farming. In his childhood, his father faced financial ruin, and the family must have been very short of money. As an adult, he seems to have been careful to build his family's wealth and status, and to hang on to it. This is important to remember when we look at his will.

Enclosures

"Open field" villages were made up of three huge fields divided into small strips, with some common land, which could be used by all for grazing. Some landowners had lots of land, some just a little, and landless laborers had none. This system could be inefficient. People could only have sheep, which was the most profitable thing to do, on the common land. People who wanted to enclose wished to break the big fields and commons up into smaller fields. Each landowner got their share of fields. The farmers who got the fields could make more money. But it also caused poverty and hardship. Poor families, without much or any land, could no longer use the common land. Farmers raised more sheep and grew less grain. This hit the poor in two ways. Farmers needed hardly any workers to look after sheep, so there were fewer jobs, and there was less grain, so the price of bread went up.

Judith's Marriage

On February 10, 1616, Shakespeare's younger daughter, Judith, married Thomas Quiney. She was 31, which was unusually old to marry. Thomas, four years younger than Judith, was not the perfect bridegroom. When he married Judith, another woman, Margaret Wheeler, was pregnant by him. She and her child both died in childbirth in March. Judith and her father may or may not have known before the wedding. They certainly knew in March, when Quiney was charged and found guilty of this crime in a church court. It may explain why Judith and Thomas were in a hurry to marry. They married in Lent when they needed a special license, just as William and Anne had.

Shakespeare's Will

At the time, people usually made their wills when they felt they were close to death. Shakespeare made a first draft of his will in January 1616. He changed it in March.[7] We don't know what the first draft said about Judith, but it is clear in March that Shakespeare didn't trust her husband, Thomas. The main provisions for her in his will were:

"unto my ~~Son in L~~ daughter Judyth"[8] – here we can see the lack of trust: *son-in-law* is crossed out, and the money left to Judith with very particular conditions: £100 ($150) to complete her dowry, £50 ($75) when she signed over her interest in the Chapel Lane cottage to Susanna, and £150 ($225), if she was alive in three years' time. This £150 ($225) was in the keeping of trustees, who would stop Thomas Quiney getting the money, only giving Judith the interest payments.

Joan Hart, his sister, got £20 ($30), all his "wearing Apparrell" (clothes) and to continue to live in the western part of the Birthplace, for a very small amount of rent. Her three sons each received £5 ($7.50).

Elizabeth Hall, his granddaughter, received "all my Plate," except a bowl that went to Judith. Plate meant his pewter and silver plates and dishes.

He gave "the Poore of Stratford" £10 ($15).

He left "to my godson William Walker" £20 ($30) in gold.

"my ffellowes John Hemynge Richard Burbage & Henry Cundell xxvjs viijd A peece to buy them Ringes." They were the only people from Shakespeare's life in the theater who are mentioned in his will.

All his property went to Susanna, **entailed** to her eldest son (if she had one), or if not, to her daughter Elizabeth, then to *her* eldest son. Clearly, Shakespeare wanted to create a single large estate that would always go to the eldest son. Susanna and her husband, John, also got "All the rest of my goodes chattels Leases plate Jewels & householde stuffe whatsoever." This included his books, and his theater shares if he had not sold them earlier.

"Item I give unto my wife my second best bed with the furniture." As you can see, this was added between two lines. Does it mean that he had forgotten her? It could, but more likely it was added here because this bequest was originally on the first page, and when the first page was copied, it was missed out. This isn't the only thing he left her. She had her **dower right** under the law to live in New Place until she died, and to one-third of the income he left to Susanna. And what about the "second best bed" part? It could have been their marriage bed. Interestingly, it could have been a bed from Anne's old home that needed to be returned.[9]

Myth Shakespeare Hated His Wife

Many biographies assume Shakespeare was forced into marriage by Anne's pregnancy, or even perhaps purposely trapped by her cunning plan. The story goes on: they soon tired of one another, and he left Stratford after a couple of years of marriage. This interpretation is reinforced by the will in which all she gets is the second-best bed—and that seems an afterthought. This is possible, but it isn't the only story that fits the facts. There really aren't many facts about their married life. Anne was pregnant when they married, and she was in Stratford when their children were born. She died in Stratford in 1623. The only other thing we know is in his will in 1601, Thomas Whittington, who had been the Hathaway's shepherd, mentioned 40 shillings "that is in the hand of Anne Shaxpere." This is often interpreted as evidence that Shakespeare left Anne short of money, and she had to borrow. It is at least as likely that Whittington left the money in her care. She was the daughter of his old master, married to the successful Mr. Shakespeare, and there were no banks at the time.

We don't know if Anne lived in Stratford or London. We don't know if the couple were miserable when they were apart, or when they were together. Perhaps William had plotted to marry Anne (she did have some money), and perhaps the creative, but careful, William depended on Anne's capable management of their lives. This fits the facts just as well.

Shakespeare's Monuments

Shakespeare died on April 23, 1616. He was buried inside the church two days later. We don't know what caused his death. His sister Joan's husband had died the week before, and some historians think there was an outbreak of the disease we call typhus in the town that month.

We've seen in his will how Shakespeare wanted to consolidate his wealth in one estate and pass it through the generations. His family decided to erect a monument suitable for the founder of a dynasty. It was made in Southwark, not far from the Globe, by Gheerart Janssen the younger. The family must have found it an acceptable likeness, because they used it in Stratford's church. This memorial bust (above) is one of only two authentic likenesses of Shakespeare. The monument hasn't had an easy history. Originally it was painted, but an 18th-century vicar whitewashed it to make it look more dignified. On October 2, 1973, thieves cut the bust out from the wall looking for hidden manuscripts. They didn't find any, and the damage has been repaired.

FACTS

June 5, 1607 Daughter Susanna marries John Hall, a doctor.
1611–12 *The Tempest* and *The Winter's Tale* are performed at court.
May 1612 Shakespeare testifies at the Belott Mountjoy case in London.
1612–3 *Cardenio* (twice), *Henry IV Part 1*, *Much Ado*, *Winter's Tale*, *Julius Caesar*, *Tempest*, and *Henry IV Part 2* are performed at court.
March 10, 1613 Shakespeare buys the Blackfriars gatehouse.
March 24, 1613 Shakespeare designs the Earl of Rutland's impressa.
June 29, 1613 The Globe burns down during a performance of *Henry VIII*.
October 28, 1614 Shakespeare does a private deal with the Welcome enclosers to protect his tithe income.
November and December 1614 Shakespeare visits London for the Christmas court performances.
February 10, 1616 His daughter Judith marries Thomas Quiney.
April 23, 1616 Shakespeare dies in Stratford.

In fact, Shakespeare did not found a dynasty. Judith's children died young. Only Elizabeth, Susanna's daughter, lived a long life. She married Thomas Nash and then Sir John Bernard. She died, childless, in 1670.

The second authentic likeness of Shakespeare comes from his second monument: the book *Mr William Shakespeare's Comedies, Histories & Tragedies: Published according to the True Originall Copies*, which is usually called the *First Folio*. The 1623 edition is called *First* because it was reprinted three times in the next 62 years, each time with small changes, and *Folio* because that was the name of the size of this large book (made by folding a full standard sheet of paper in half).

The *First Folio* is vital to Shakespeare's reputation as a literary superstar. It contains 36 of his plays and is the only reason 18 survive. These include *The Tempest, Twelfth Night, Julius Caesar,* and *Macbeth*. John Heminges and Henry Condell, his fellow sharers and housekeepers, collected and arranged the publication of these "true originall copies." The King's Men owned the plays, and Heminges and Condell used the company's own manuscripts.

Shakespeare's Reputation

Parliament shut all theaters in England in 1642, and they did not open again until 1660. In the 25 years between Shakespeare's death and the closure, he was not the literary superstar that he is now. His plays continued to be performed, but others were more popular. For example, we know the titles of many of the plays performed at court. During these 25 years, 16 were Shakespeare's, but 50 were by Fletcher (often with a collaborator). However, as others' reputations diminished, Shakespeare's grew.

Epilogue

How do we sum up Shakespeare? Some consistent themes come through the story we have been looking at.

He was steeped in the theater—as an actor, a playwright, a company sharer, and part owner of two theaters. You can't make a convincing historical case for Shakespeare not writing the plays. There's too much evidence that he did. His connections with the theater and plays at court, how his wealth grew, the repeated references to him as a playwright, all fit together. Historians evaluate their evidence, and then follow it. The only way anybody can argue Shakespeare didn't write the plays is by saying it was a conspiracy, that everybody else at the time was fooled, and Shakespeare was paid to pretend to be the author. This isn't history. It is the worst kind of unsupported inference or invention. It is like a conspiracy theory, with the same lack of factual basis as stories about alien abductions or the existence of unicorns.

This is from the play-within-the-play in *A Midsummer Night's Dream*. Bottom (playing Pyramus) tries to kiss Flute (playing Thisbe) through a hole in the wall (played by Snout). It is one of those moments that suggest the author knew exactly what worked on stage.

Shakespeare was careful with money, and determined to die a rich man, leaving a significant estate to his (hopefully male) descendants. He wasn't a perfect person. The idea of a "role model" is a modern one—another anachronism. It would be nice to think of Shakespeare as caring and daring, but in his financial dealings, he can seem selfish. If he did change his story in the Belott Mountjoy case, he abandoned Belott and his wife, Mary. He did less than most other prominent citizens of Stratford to help the poor in the Welcome enclosure case.

We have lots of evidence about Shakespeare, but most of the time it doesn't tell us what we want to know. When we don't know, we must accept this, not speculate or invent. Shakespeare's books are a good example. Scholars have tracked dozens of books he must have read, because he quotes from them, or they clearly influence what he wrote. Yet there are no books mentioned in his will. But then the inventory of his goods that went with the will is lost, and everything went to Susanna and John Hall, so there was no need to mention individual items. So the correct conclusion is not that he had no books, but that we don't know what books he had.

Myth   The Earl of Oxford Wrote Shakespeare's Plays

Why don't I, the author, believe the Earl of Oxford wrote the plays?

- The idea that Shakespeare wasn't educated enough because he didn't go to university is erroneous. We saw, when we looked at his schooling, that the Elizabethan grammar school gave an extensive classical education. Students had to read, write, and learn by heart Latin text.
- The idea that he didn't travel enough, or mix in high enough society to write the plays is also a mistake. It is part of the mistake of thinking the plays are autobiographical. They are works of the imagination. Shakespeare could mix with all sorts of people in London, and he had access to a wide range of books.
- Oxford died on June 24, 1604. Fifteen of the plays were written after this, and as we have seen, many fit in with the changes in politics and the new indoor theater.
- The plays show a consistent understanding of what works on stage and a development of skill and technique. This fits the facts of the life of the actor and theatrical shareholder William Shakespeare, not the aristocratic Earl of Oxford.

Timeline

1564	Born *c.* April 23, Stratford, Warwickshire, England
1576	The Theatre, London's first permanent playhouse, opens
1582	*c.* November 28, marries Anne Hathaway
1583	May 26, daughter Susanna Shakespeare baptized
1584	First English colonists land at Roanoke in Virginia
1585	February 2, twins Hamnet and Judith Shakespeare baptized
1592	March 3, *Henry VI Part 1* first performed at the Rose Theatre
	September 20, criticized in Greene's *Groats-worth of Witte*
1593	February, poem *Venus and Adonis* published
1594	May, poem *The Rape of Lucrece* published
	Becomes a sharer in the Lord Chamberlain's Men
1596	Christmas, *Henry IV Part 1* performed at court
1597	November 15, listed as not having paid his taxes
1598	February 4, listed as having 80 bushels of malt in Stratford
	September 7, Francis Meres praises Shakespeare's poems and plays
	October 1, listed as having not paid a tax bill
1599	Moves to Bankside in London
	Summer, the Globe Theatre opens with Shakespeare as a shareholder
1603	February 2, *Midsummer Night's Dream* performed at court
	March, Elizabeth I dies, James I becomes King of England
	May 17, Shakespeare's company becomes the King's Men
1604	Shakespeare is living in Silver Street in London
	March 15, Shakespeare and King's Men in the coronation procession
	In Stratford, sells Philip Rogers 20 bushels of malt on credit
1605	July 24, buys a half interest in tithes outside Stratford
	November 5, Gunpowder Plot fails
1607	June 5, daughter Susanna marries John Hall, a doctor
1608	August 17, sues Richard Addenbroke of Stratford for debt
1611–12	*The Tempest* and *The Winter's Tale* performed at court
1612	May, testifies at the Belott Mountjoy case in London
1612–13	*Cardenio, Henry IV Part 1, Much Ado, The Winter's Tale, Julius Caesar, Tempest, Henry IV Part 2* performed at court
1613	March 10, buys the Blackfriars Gatehouse
	March 24, designs the Earl of Rutland's "impressa"
	June 29, the Globe burns down during a performance of *Henry VIII*
1614	October 28, makes deal with the Welcome enclosers to protect tithe income
	November and December, in London
1616	February 10, daughter Judith marries Thomas Quiney in Stratford
	April 23, dies in Stratford
1623	*First Folio* published

Money Then and Now

The table below picks out some prices and wages from around 1600, during Shakespeare's lifetime, and compares them with current prices and wages. The central section shows you the 1600 price multiplied by the figure at the top of the column. So 1d (one penny) multiplied by 200 would be 83 pence, multiplied by 300 would be £1.25, and so on. The figures in bold show you the best comparison between prices then and now. As you can see, no single multiplier gives an accurate conversion to current prices, even for this small range of things. Most people, including children, drank beer as their normal drink. Tea and coffee were unknown, and water was not always safe to drink. Today, £1 is equal to about $1.50 in U.S. currency.

| | c. 1600 | Multiply by | | | | | | | 2013 price |
		200	300	500	800	2000	3000	5000	
pint of beer	½ d	£0.42	£0.63	£1.04	£1.67	**£4.17**	£6.25	£10.42	£3.50
loaf of bread	1d	**£0.83**	**£1.25**	£2.08	£3.33	£8.33	£12.50	£20.83	85p–£1.35
cheapest entry, Globe	1d	£0.83	£1.25	£2.08	£3.33	£8.33	**£12.50**	£20.83	£12.00
cheapest entry, Blackfriars	6d	£5.00	£7.50	£12.50	**£20.00**	£50.00	£75.00	£125.00	£25.00
book of a new play	6d	£5.00	**£7.50**	£12.50	£20.00	£50.00	£75.00	£125.00	£9.99
rent a horse/ car for a day	12d	£10.00	£15.00	**£25.00**	**£40.00**	£100.00	£150.00	£250.00	£33.66
copy of the First Folio	£1	**£200.00**	£300.00	£500.00	£800.00	£2,000.00	£3,000.00	£5,000.00	£150.00
Salaries									
Baker	£4 13s 6d	£935	£1,403	£2,338	£3,740	£9,350	£14,025	**£23,375**	£24,000
Stratford school master /modern headteacher	£20	£4,000	£6,000	£10,000	£16,000	£40,000	£60,000	**£100,000**	£85–100,000

Glossary

abdicate when a monarch gives up their throne

apprentice youth who has a contract to learn a trade

armory place where weapons and armor are stored

auditorium part of a theater where the audience is

banns announcement that a marriage is planned, giving time to object for any person who knows a reason why it should not be allowed

birch bundle of sticks used for beating people

bond money that is paid as security for something

capital large sums of money saved or invested

court household of the monarch, including government ministers, and everyone who lived and worked there

discovery space central opening in the tiring house wall at the back of the stage which could be opened to reveal things to the audience

doublet jacket with removable sleeves

dower right right of a widow to live in the family home and have one-third of her dead husband's income

dowry property or money the bride's family gives to the husband

empathy ability to see another person's point of view

entail legal procedure to leave an inheritance to particular heirs (for example, the eldest son in each generation) and to stop it being broken up

epilogue section at the end of a play or book that acts as a conclusion

executor person responsible for seeing a will is carried out as the dead person intended

favorite adviser given many gifts by the king, often more than their service is worth

gable triangular upper part of a wall at the end of a roof

gallery (usually three) tiers of seats in a playhouse

guild company of people from the same trade who regulate the way the trade can be carried out

heresy religious belief which is against the beliefs of the state church

hierarchical organized by class from the top (king) to the lowest (homeless beggar)

holy day a saint's day; in Shakespeare's time, these were public holidays.

housekeeper in Shakespeare's theater, a shareholder in a theater building

infer to come to a conclusion by using reasoning rather than facts

Jacobean from the reign of James I

lath and plaster strips of wood, plastered on the outside, used to make walls and ceilings in buildings

lease legal document renting property for a given number of years

lutenist person who plays the lute, a stringed instrument

Muses in Greek myths, the nine goddesses of the Arts

original practices style of production pioneered at Shakespeare's Globe by Mark Rylance and his team to re-create the costume and music Shakespeare's audiences would have recognized

parish small district with its own church and clergy; sometimes a unit of local government based on it

patron person who gives support or protection, often financial

pirate edition book printed and sold by people who did not have the right to do so

polygonal many-sided

Puritan strict Protestant in religion, somebody who wanted a more godly society, with rules enforcing good behavior

Reformation change in official Church from Roman Catholic to Protestant; at the time, all people in the country were forced to worship only in the official Church.

rhetoric using words persuasively; also can be used to describe exaggerated language

royal patent permission given by a monarch to an acting company, allowing them to perform

sharer in English theater from 1576 to 1642, a shareholder in a company of players

shroud cloth a dead person is wrapped in for burial

Shrove short for Shrovetide, the three days in the Christian calendar before the start of Lent; a time for merrymaking and excess in Shakespeare's time.

slander in law, to speak lies about another person

soliloquy speech by an actor directly to the audience, usually about feelings or plans

sonnet 14-line poem with a set rhyme scheme

speculator one who makes risky investments hoping for large profits

stage trap trapdoor in the stage that could be opened to let devils enter, be a grave, and so on

sturdy beggar legal description of a person who was fit to work, but was begging, not working

synonym word with the same or similar meaning as another word

tenant person renting a property

tiring house in England from 1576 to 1642, the part of the theater behind the stage, where the actors dressed and waited to go on stage, and where the companies' play books and costumes were stored

treason in law, the crime of betraying your country or monarch

usurer person who lends money for interest, which is usually high

wherry light rowing boat that acted as a water taxi on the River Thames

whittawer somebody who tanned leather and dealt in luxury goods

Source References

Who Was Shakespeare? (4–5)

1. www.telegraph.co.uk/comment/columnists/borisjohnson/8600125/Shakespeare-torchbearer-for-the-Chinese-way-of-doing-things.html [accessed February 9, 2013].
2. Elise Broach, *Shakespeare's Secret* (London: Walker Books, 2006) 42. I owe this reference to the best modern account of the controversy about who wrote the plays, James Shapiro's *Contested Will: Who wrote Shakespeare?* (London: Faber and Faber, 2010).

Where Did Shakespeare Come From? (6–12)

1. S. Schoenbaum, *William Shakespeare: A Documentary Life* (Oxford: OUP, 1975), 13–15. The fine is in the records of the Stratford Town Council.
2. *Ibid*, 18; shaksper.net/archive/2005/225-march/22532-john-jordans-book.
3. *Ibid*, 24; and Bill Bryson, *Shakespeare: The World as a Stage* (London: Harper Perennial, 2008), 23–4.
4. You can see the page at findingshakespeare.co.uk/going-digital-the-birth-and-burial-records-of-william-shakespeare/sbt_bs_ws36_dr243_1_p2.
5. Bill Bryson, *Shakespeare: The World as a Stage*, 37–8.
6. *Ibid*, 38

After School...Marriage (12–17)

1. S. Schoenbaum, *William Shakespeare: A Documentary Life*, 36–8; and Stephen Greenblatt, *Will in the World* (London: Jonathan Cape, 2004), 57–60.
2. S. Schoenbaum, *William Shakespeare: A Documentary Life*, 41.
3. *Ibid*, 46
4. *Ibid*, 62
5. *Ibid*, 70. The original is in Latin.
6. *Ibid*, 63. The original is in Latin.
7. Bill Bryson, *Shakespeare: The World as a Stage*, 40.
8. Stephen Greenblatt, *Will in the World*, 118–19; and S. Schoenbaum, *William Shakespeare: A Documentary Life*, 75–6.

What Happened Next? (18–21)

1. The earliest versions of this story are tracked down in S. Schoenbaum, *William Shakespeare: A Compact Documentary Life*, 97–99. Michael Wood, *In Search of Shakespeare* (London: BBC Books, 2005), 106–8, looks at how the story might contain a grain of truth.
2. Quoted in Michael Wood, *In Search of Shakespeare*, 59.

Moving to London (22–33)

1. This is based on a translation by Clare Williams. To read Platter's full account of his time in England see Peter Razzell, ed., *The Journals of Two Travellers in Elizabethan and Early Stuart England* (London: Caliban Books, 1995).
2. Julian Bowsher, *Shakespeare's London Theatreland* (London: Museum of London Archaeology, 2012), 68–80.
3. S. Schoenbaum, *William Shakespeare: A Documentary Life*, 116.
4. In *Kind Heart's Dream*, 1592, quoted in S. Schoenbaum, *William Shakespeare: A Documentary Life*, 117.
5. R.A. Foakes, *Henslowe's Diary, 2nd ed.* (Cambridge: CUP, 2002), 16–9.
6. Michael Wood, *In Search of Shakespeare*, 149, estimates 1,634 in the galleries, and says that should be more than doubled to allow for the yard. So my calculation is: over 30,000 saw the play, and the population of London was 200,000 (see note 1 on page 22).
7. E.K. Chambers, *The Elizabethan Stage*, 4 vols (Oxford: Clarendon Press, 1945), IV, 199.
8. S. Schoenbaum, *William Shakespeare: A Compact Documentary Life*, 126.
9. For the different theaters in London, and where they were, see Jane Shuter, *Shakespeare and the Theatre* (Oxford: Raintree, 2014), 11; and Wendy Greenhill, *Shakespeare's Theatre, 2nd ed.* (Oxford: Heinemann, 2007), 5–19.

What Makes Shakespeare Different? (34–43)

1. S. Schoenbaum, *William Shakespeare: A Documentary Life*, 140.
2. Robert Parker Sorlien, ed., *The Diary of John Manningham of the Middle Temple, 1602–1603*, (Boston: University Press of New England, 1976), 75.
3. For a fuller description of problems posed by the sonnets, see Bryson, *Shakespeare: The World as a Stage*, 137–46 and Michael Wood, *In Search of*

Shakespeare, 188–200.

4. S. Schoenbaum, *William Shakespeare: A Documentary Life*, 140–1.

5. special-1.bl.uk/treasures/SiqDiscovery/ui/record.aspx?Source=text&LHCopy=96&LHPage=80&RHCopy=96&RHPage=81.

6. *King John*, Act 3, Scene 3, lines 95–6.

7. To find out more about this read Laurie Maguire and Emma Smith, *30 Great Myths About Shakespeare* (Oxford: Wiley-Blackwell, 2013), 113–18.

8. For a map of London's theaters see Jane Shuter, *Shakespeare and the Theatre* (Raintree, 2014), p. 11.

9. S. Schoenbaum, *William Shakespeare: A Documentary Life*, 153.

10. This is based on a translation by Clare Williams. To read Platter's full account of his time in England see Peter Razzell, ed., *The Journals of Two Travellers in Elizabethan and Early Stuart England*, (London: Caliban Books, 1995).

11. S. Schoenbaum, *William Shakespeare: A Documentary Life*, 160.

Was Shakespeare Rich? (44–49)

1. S. Schoenbaum, *William Shakespeare: A Documentary Life*, 153.

2. *Ibid*, 166–171.

3. *Ibid*, 171–3.

4. I am grateful to Philip Hall, agricultural valuer at Savills Banbury office, for the modern valuation.

5. S. Schoenbaum, *William Shakespeare: A Documentary Life*, 161–3.

6. *Ibid*, 179, 184

7. *Ibid*, 192

The King's Man (50–59)

1. E.K. Chambers, *The Elizabethan Stage*, II, 208.

2. S. Schoenbaum, *William Shakespeare: A Documentary Life*, 196.

3. Words in quotes are Shakespeare's, either from his testimony, or the testimony of Daniel Nicholas about his conversation with Shakespeare. From Charles Nicholl, *The Lodger: Shakespeare on Silver Street* (London: Allen Lane, 2007), 288–90.

4. I owe the idea, and the example, to Stephen Greenblatt, *Will in the World*, 323–9.

Did Shakespeare Retire? (60–69)

1. *The Tempest*, Act 5, Scene 1, lines 46–7, 53–56.

2. The play was originally published with a subtitle, *The Woman's Prize or the Tamer Tamed*. It has been rescued from neglect in the 21st century, with a production at the Royal Shakespeare Company (RSC) in 2003, and two modern editions of the play. All three reversed the title, calling the play *The Tamer Tamed*, because its connection to *The Taming of the Shrew* is good marketing.

3. S. Schoenbaum, William Shakespeare: *A Documentary Life*, 147–52; Andrew Gurr, *The Shakespeare Company* (Cambridge University Press, 2004), 60.

4. E.K. Chambers, *The Elizabethan Stage*, II, 419–20.

5. Charles Nicholl, *The Lodger: Shakespeare on Silver Street*, 38.

6. From a letter written on behalf of the Stratford Town Council, S. Schoenbaum, *William Shakespeare: A Documentary Life*, 230.

7. Studies of Shakespeare's will suggest he made a second draft in March, when the whole first page was written again, and by a copying mistake January was left as the date. Pages two and three just had some crossings out, and additions written between the existing lines. S. Schoenbaum, *William Shakespeare: A Documentary Life*, 242–6.

8. All words in quotation marks are direct quotes from his will, S. Schoenbaum, *William Shakespeare: A Documentary Life*, 242–5.

9. In his will, Anne's father, Richard Hathaway, mentions two beds: "Item ... the two joined-beds in my parlour, shall continue and stand unmoved during the natural life ... of Joan my wife, and the natural life of Bartholomew my son, and John my son, and the longest liver of them." So these beds were Hathaway heirlooms. Perhaps Anne had taken one to Stratford? There was only one in the Hathaway house in an inventory taken when Bartholomew died in 1624, but two again when the descendants of Richard finally left the house in the 19th century. If Anne had taken one of these beds, it would need to be clear in the will it should not go to Susanna with all the other furniture. So this clause might have been included because Anne remembered and wanted it in. This is a nice story, and obviously speculation – but no more speculation than the interpretation that sees the second-best bed as intentional rudeness from William to Anne. Michael Wood, *In Search of Shakespeare*, 374–5.

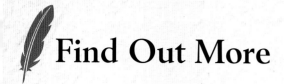

Find Out More

Books

Foster, Brett. *Shakespeare's Life*. New York: Chelsea House, 2012.

Greenhill, Wendy. *Shakespeare: Man of the Theater*. Chicago: Heinemann Library, 2000.

Kesselring, Mari. *How to Analyze the Works of William Shakespeare*. Minneapolis, MN: ABDO, 2013.

Robson, David. *Shakespeare's Globe Theater*. San Diego, CA: Reference Point Press, 2013.

Shuter, Jane. *Shakespeare and the Theater*. London: Raintree, 2014.

Web Sites

www.folger.edu

For more information on Shakespeare's works, Elizabethan theater, and links to Shakespeare's poems, sonnets, and films of his plays. You can also visit the library, located in Washington, D.C., and view its collection of Shakespeare-related material.

www.shakespeare.org.uk

Learn more about Shakespeare's life and the times he lived in.

Shakespeare Onstage

The best way to appreciate the work of William Shakespeare is to see his plays performed live onstage. For a complete listing of Shakespeare festivals and theaters, visit **www.shakespearefellowship.org/linksfestivals.htm**

Index